peaceful gardens

Stephanie Donaldson
with photography by Melanie Eclare

peaceful gardens

transform your garden into a haven of calm and tranquillity

RYLAND
PETERS
& SMALL

LONDON NEW YORK

For Ben

For this edition:

Designer Sonya Nathoo

Senior editor Clare Double

Picture researcher
Emily Westlake

Production Deborah Wehner

Art director Ann-Marie Bulat

Editorial director Julia Charles

First published in the United Kingdom in 2003
This compact version published in 2006
by Ryland Peters & Small, Inc.
519 Broadway, 5th Floor
New York, NY 10012

www.rylandpeters.com

10 9 8 7 6 5 4 3 2 1

Text © 2003, 2005 Stephanie Donaldson
Design and photographs © 2003, 2005
Ryland Peters & Small
The following photographs © Steve Painter: 96r, 97

ISBN-10: 1-84597-099-3
ISBN-13: 978-1-84597-099-4

The hardback edition of this book
was cataloged as follows:

Library of Congress Cataloging-in-
Publication Data

Donaldson, Stephanie.
  Peaceful gardens : transform your
garden into a haven of calm and
tranquillity / Stephanie Donaldson.
    p. cm.
Includes index.
  ISBN 1-84172-388-6
  1. Gardens–Design. 2. Landscape
gardening. I. Title.
  SB473 .D65 2003
  712'.6–dc21
                        2002012956

Printed and bound in China

contents

We live in a stressful world where we all need a haven, a place to forget our usual concerns—somewhere we can be simple, re-establish our place in the natural order of things, and experience contentment, even if it is only for a few moments. There are people who lose themselves in books; others find physical exercise is the key, but for true contentment there is little to rival time spent in a garden. The fears and frustrations of life soon recede when there is direct contact with nature.

introduction

How you choose to spend your time in the garden is very much a matter of personal preference. It may be that you are never happier than when you are ambling along behind your lawnmower, while someone else may choose to lie in a hammock and gaze at the sky through a canopy of leaves, and others will find true contentment by growing their own vegetables. Your choice will inevitably dictate your garden's appearance, but before making any changes it is always wise to separate the achievable dreams from the fantasies. The French "potager" at Villandry is a glory to behold, but it is also extremely work-intensive, and the opportunities to take your ease in a garden of this kind are few and far between. However, a modest vegetable plot tucked behind a picket fence can be decorative, productive, and a peaceful place.

opposite **In a quiet corner, the soft colors of the ivy-clad wall make a backdrop to an elegant antique bench, which looks comfortably inviting with its flowery yet restrained cushions.**

Consider carefully before you embark on creating your dream garden—small changes can be as effective as grand designs.

A peaceful garden—simple or harmonious to look at, restful to sit in—is a place of balance, sufficiently demanding of your time to be satisfying without enslaving you. It's the place where you can be your true self, relaxed and at ease—a place where you feel free to be sad, happy, or even a little sentimental. In the peaceful garden, listening to the song of a bird or smelling a rose is as important as weeding; it should touch all the senses and leave you feeling enriched. In the most literal way, you can "earth" yourself by putting your hands in the soil. So many of life's experiences today are indirect—our food often comes from the other side of the planet; the music we listen to is recorded; we communicate via telephone, fax, or e-mail—so when we cultivate the soil and plant a seed or seedling, nurture it, and watch it grow, the wonder and satisfaction we feel are very precious.

left An apparently carefree, informal garden demands a gardener who is happy with a degree of untidiness. To keep it in flower throughout the growing season is an endless task—far better to accept that it has its high spots, and sit back and relax at other times, leaving the plants to set seed and provide continuity in the years ahead. This style of garden is for those who work with nature rather than those who seek to control it.

peaceful shapes and spaces

keeping it simple

symmetry and balance

contemplation and relaxation

special places

"Peace" is a word that engages heart and head—we feel it with our emotions as we understand it with our intellect. This is a central element in the creation of a successful peaceful garden. When considering any aspect of the design, check your emotional response to your plans as well as practical aspects. Remember you are seeking a calming rather than a stimulating effect.

keeping it simple

Simplicity is key. Often the starting point is what is removed rather than what is added. Taking away fussy detail and clutter and restricting the color palette has an immediate calming effect that is both visually and emotionally satisfying. This is true of the plants as well as the solid elements contained within the garden.

right **Concealing the labor-intensive vegetable garden behind a woven fence allows the gardener to sit and enjoy the view without being lured from a quiet, restful moment by any task that needs doing.**

below **Wide, shallow steps—the treads and margins softened by plants—lead to a mown path that curves invitingly away into the distance. Matching the width of the path to the steps creates a generous avenue for a companionable stroll.**

A garden is not just what happens within its boundaries—it is also profoundly influenced by its surroundings. Understanding these additional influences will help you create the peaceful, calming retreat you desire.

Where a garden is bordered by open countryside, distant views, other mature gardens, or parkland, it should take advantage of what is known by designers as the "borrowed view." Allow the space to flow into its surroundings, using the landscape to lift and lead the eye to the wider view. Conversely, if buildings or unattractive features are visible from the garden, or it is enclosed by trees with no view beyond, concentrate on the inner view. Keep focal points at low levels so that the eye is engaged by what is within the garden's boundaries and does not look upward and outward. In either case, the eye should travel smoothly across what it sees rather than jumping from spot to spot.

When making use of the wider view, remember that it will be most effective if you resist making the garden itself too busy. Large areas of grass, some mown, some left to grow long, with a few carefully positioned trees, will lead seamlessly to the view beyond. It is no accident that in many historic gardens the perennial beds and potagers are contained within walls or hedges. Their impact is all the greater when confined, and so positioned they do not detract from the surrounding landscape. In a small garden which benefits from a good view, a similar effect can be achieved by restricting borders and structures to the area closest to the house, gradually paring down the planting and hard landscaping so that at the end of the space, adjacent to the view, the garden is at its simplest and least contrived.

Unlike the owners of the great gardens, most people who live in the country do not have a belt of parkland separating them from the more

industrial aspects of agriculture—fields left uncultivated, muddy pastures, or functional farm buildings—so it is generally advisable to have an informal boundary between the garden and the fields beyond. A mixed hedge of indigenous shrubs and trees works well—especially if one or two trees are allowed to grow tall and frame the view. Selective pruning of this type of boundary can work wonders (left untrimmed it is a barrier); cut lower in places to open up a view or echo the curves of the landscape beyond, it becomes part of the bigger picture.

Where a fence is necessary it is best kept low, rustic in appearance, and preferably open, above right The tiniest garden—a windowsill, balcony, or terrace—can contain miniature landscapes of great subtlety. Here, a leaf-shaped carved rock emerges from a bed of gravel. Carefully positioned succulents complete the picture.

below right A shallow bowl emulates the arid landscape where these succulents grow naturally. The mulch of pebbles is functional as well as decorative, preventing soil from splashing onto the leaves during watering.

opposite The uncluttered simplicity of this courtyard is reminiscent of a Japanese temple or a monastic cloister. The grass growing in the central stone block is the only touch of green.

Where good views are absent, the peaceful garden needs to exclude the world beyond its boundaries. It is a more intimate and enclosed space, and sometimes consists of little more than a tabletop display, a balcony, or a courtyard.

such as a simple rail fence. This type of fence can always be made animal- or childproof by attaching wire netting, while still retaining the view beyond.

In less rural surroundings, privacy becomes a major consideration. However fabulous the borrowed view, if it opens the garden to passersby or neighbors, some screening will be necessary or its peacefulness may be compromised. A fence topped by trellis through which plants can twine both conceals and reveals the view beyond. A tall hedge neatly trimmed into undulating curves rather than a horizontal line can be used to frame the best of

above A rooftop terrace is sheltered from the wind and hidden from a nearby apartment building by large-scale but simple planting that is in harmony with the minimalist architecture and furniture.

left An urban garden keeps planting to a minimum and relies on sculptural shapes and dramatic lighting for impact—this is somewhere to look at rather than a place in which to relax. Although low maintenance, this type of garden needs regular attention to make sure the gravel stays free of fallen leaves and weeds, or it quickly looks neglected.

the view while masking most of the garden from the outside. Seasonal screening in the form of deciduous trees, shrubs, and climbers provides privacy in the summer months when the garden is most used, yet opens views during the rest of the year. This type of garden can be both inward and outward looking, depending on the season.

In urban or other situations where good views are absent, the peaceful garden needs to exclude the world beyond its boundaries. It is a more intimate and enclosed space, and sometimes consists of little more than a carefully arranged tabletop display, a balcony, or a courtyard. Here in particular, it is the atmosphere rather than the dimensions of the garden that creates the mood. Although a barrier of trees and shrubs seems the obvious way to separate the garden from its surroundings, this can sometimes prove problematic in an urban environment. If you are overlooked by tall buildings and buffeted by gusts of wind, it may prove difficult to establish the plants, and where they do grow successfully, the result can be a dank, damp, and shady garden with sour soil. In this situation the hard landscaping needs to be strong and well conceived, creating focal points and harmonious shapes that draw the eye so the planting becomes less central. A few carefully chosen architectural plants will have far more impact and be easier to take care of than a motley selection of undemanding shrubs tolerant of urban conditions.

It is particularly important to relate form to function in the urban garden. However beautifully designed a garden is, if it can't be used the way its owner envisaged, it is a failure. The conflicting emotions that result will be far from peaceful. It is important to ask yourself how you plan to make use of your garden before embarking on any changes, and any good garden designer will ask you detailed questions about what you want from your garden before redesigning it.

Different people want different things. Some city dwellers want nothing more than a beautiful, undemanding space to look out on. They have neither the time nor the inclination to garden. They simply want a place that is soothing to look at at the end of a stressful day. This minimalist style of garden is very much the province of childless urbanites. A family would find that it caused more conflict than harmony when children scattered such a garden with toys or grazed their

right **Careful pruning has revealed the sculptural shape of the tree that shades this city garden. Rather than attempting to grow other plants, which would dilute its impact and possibly struggle to survive in its shade, the designer has created textured horizontal surfaces on two levels. A simple trellis fence encloses the garden, giving it some privacy without depriving it of borrowed light. A vase of sunflowers adds a temporary splash of color.**

knees on raked gravel surfaces, and an avid gardener would soon grow frustrated by the lack of plants. While most people will fill a balcony or terrace with plants, others see it as an outdoor room that needs nothing more than a few carefully chosen pieces of furniture. It may irritate friends and family who long to decorate the space with plants, but if a sparsely furnished outdoor room is your idea of a peaceful garden, outsiders should not be allowed to interfere.

These days, when many of us work from home, our gardens have a new role. Any part of the garden that leads from a work space needs to be restful to look at, but not necessarily inviting or it will prove a distraction. In my own case, the view from my desk is of treetops and sky—good for gazing at while I think, but not directly engaging. Initially I had planned to put my desk in another room where there is a view of the sea, but I realized that I would never get any work done. The ever-changing moods of the sea and the

above **Folding chairs and a couple of rustic tables beckon invitingly, the perfect setting for a summer meal in the garden. It's tempting to imagine that the tethered goats are four-legged lawnmowers; but as they are more browsers than grazers, they will probably be more interested in the food on the table.**

left **The curving slate wall defines and separates the different areas in this garden designed by Roberto Silva. At the far end, wooden decking creates a spacious outdoor room simply furnished with a table and chairs.**

keeping it simple **21**

comings and goings of the fishing boats would have proved far more interesting than the task at hand. For work spaces in particular, keep the outlook simple. Avoid fussy details or planting—a single well-tended plant or tree is more appropriate than a bed full of flowers that will lure you out to deadhead or prune.

When it comes to planting, simplicity and restraint are more calming than busy beds incorporating single specimens of numerous varieties. If you are a plant enthusiast, it is easy to get carried away and end up with something that is more plant zoo than garden as you strive to include every plant that takes your fancy. When making a peaceful garden, temper this tendency and adopt a "less is more" approach. This is true of color, too—the use of a limited palette is more soothing to the eye than a vibrant mixture, which can easily be overstimulating and is definitely not tranquil in its effect. Avoid combining colors that intensify one another and choose instead those that blend subtly together. Anyone familiar with the English countryside will know that the different shades and shapes of green that make up its meadows and woodlands create a supremely beautiful and peaceful environment. On a smaller scale, this use of subtle shades rather than contrasting colors can have the same effect.

In a rural garden, using improved cultivars of the wildflowers that grow locally, in natural-looking drifts, will create a seamless blend with the countryside beyond. Cultivars feature the best qualities of the wildflower, but frequently have larger blooms and longer flowering periods. Be cautious in your use of

opposite left **Planting that echoes the local flora can link a country garden to the landscape. In this garden, large swathes of** *Geranium phaeum* **fill the foreground, and pathways zigzag their way toward the graceful arching branches of a** *Buddleia alternifolia*.

opposite right **A path mown through a meadow brings you close to the beauty of the grasses without trampling them. The play of light on the grass creates an ever-changing mood.**

below **Inspired planting at a garden created by Peter and Pam Lewis. The russet-pink haze of flowering cloud grass is punctuated by the lollipop heads of** *Allium cristophii* **and pink pincushion flowers. The dried seedheads will add interest later in the year.**

Water is a wonderful addition. Keep the garden tranquil with rills that flow imperceptibly or still pools that reflect their surroundings. Keep shapes simple —rectangles, squares, and circles.

true wildflowers unless they are from an assured source; plundering the local flora is no way to create a peaceful garden.

In a garden with large areas of lawn, a mown path can be very appealing as it curves sinuously through the long grass. The sight of long grass rippling in the wind has a quiet beauty that rivals the colorful displays of flowers in many cultivated gardens.

Leaf shape and plant outline are elements that should be considered when planning a garden. This doesn't necessarily mean that you should always seek out plants with rounded leaves and gentle curves, but that the plants you choose should enhance the atmosphere of the garden. In a minimalist garden, a plant with architectural foliage is more appropriate than a rose—however beautiful the rose may be, it will look out of place and feel discordant in such a setting.

These days, it seems that no garden is complete unless it has a water feature of some sort, and there is no doubt that, used correctly, water is a wonderful addition to a peaceful garden. A gently bubbling fountain becomes a focal point, and you will become lost in a world of your own as you listen to its soothing sound and watch the movement of the water. Remember, however, that fast-moving water has an energizing effect, which may disrupt the contemplative mood. Avoid anything that splashes noisily or flows at a hectic pace—keep the

right A rill of water flows gently across an urban roof terrace in a shallow galvanized metal trough. Stones in the water echo the pebbles that surround it, and a corkscrew willow casts dappled shadows.

far right Still water acts like a mirror, reflecting the surrounding trees and the sky above. Try to avoid overhanging branches, though, or your pool will be filled with brown leaves in the fall.

left By limiting the palette of colors you use in a garden you can calm the effect of a complex planting scheme. The various shapes, shades, and textures in this formal front garden create a pleasing green tapestry. Slight touches of other colors highlight the general theme. Color-themed gardens are always most effective when other colors make subtle appearances; otherwise, the effect can be dull.

garden tranquil with rills that flow imperceptibly or still pools that reflect their surroundings. Keep the shapes simple—rectangles, squares, or circles rather than the peculiar amorphous shapes that still seem to be strangely popular. Don't forget the practicalities either. When installing water features in a garden, it is always advisable to consult an expert—few things can spoil the mood of a space more effectively than a poorly installed pond that turns murky green at the drop of a hat and requires endless maintenance. If the complexities of pumps and filters, wiring, and water supplies all prove too expensive and time-consuming, you can emulate the Chinese and grow waterlilies in large, water-filled, glazed pots. Waterlilies love deep, still water and will grow happily this way, especially if they are in partial shade. Choose a small-growing or miniature variety, or divide the plant every other year.

Small or large, inward or outward looking, every garden needs somewhere to sit. Bear in mind that the style of seating and the materials used for the hard landscaping should relate to the rest of the garden. Concrete paving slabs look fine in a contemporary urban garden, and a wooden deck is entirely appropriate in a waterfront site, but used elsewhere they sometimes have a tendency to look uncomfortably out of place. When peacefulness is the aim, these dissonant associations should be avoided. Seating, too, should be chosen with care—but in choosing a suitable style, don't get so carried away by the aesthetic that you end up with something that is wonderful to look at but impossibly uncomfortable. Remember form *and* function—*and* simplicity.

symmetry and balance

Consider the difference between symmetry and balance within the peaceful garden. Symmetry mirrors one side of the garden with the other, while balance combines differing features in a pleasing way. Symmetry can be achieved intellectually; balance requires feeling.

left **The dark surface of the circular pond acts as a mirror, reflecting light from the sky above and creating new perspectives. Almost lost against the backdrop of the sago palm in its green planter, the flowering spike of the acanthus gains definition in the reflection.**

above **Pairs of boxwood cones contribute to the symmetry of this formal garden. They also help lift the eye from the strong horizontals of the pond, stone, and clipped hedges.**

Most people have a preference for either symmetry or balance. Symmetry is more ordered and predictable; balance can be fluid or curvaceous. If you are uncertain which you prefer, the photographs in this book may help you decide—do you instinctively favor formal regularity, or does a more free-form garden appeal to you? When you are deciding whether to follow the symmetrical or the balanced route, it is also important to take the shape of your garden into consideration. The garden must sit comfortably within its boundaries. It is much trickier to achieve symmetry in an area that is asymmetrical in shape than in a neatly rectangular yard, and it is equally difficult to ignore the influence of the geometry on this shape of garden if you have something less formal in mind. Either way, bear in mind that your intuition is often the best guide, and it is only when something clearly isn't working that this type of analysis comes in useful.

The guiding principle of the symmetrical garden is the mirroring of one side by the other. Angles match, paths are central or flanking the center; and with the exception of the placing of a large object as a focal point at the end of a vista, this type of ornamentation is used in pairs. When it works, symmetry is emotionally and visually satisfying, but when it isn't quite right, the result can induce anxiety rather than calm—something to be avoided in a peaceful garden.

Planning helps; with the aid of a ruler and a drawing square (or garden-design software), drawing a symmetrical garden on paper is not difficult. Even if you have never done this type of thing before, you will quickly see if the proposed shapes sit well with one another. Doing this also reveals an intriguing aspect of the symmetrical garden. While it should be divided into two even halves across its width, if the same is done lengthwise, the proportions seldom work, nor if it is divided into quarters. If necessary, it should be divided into thirds.

left The formality of the clipped bay trees and their wooden tubs is an interesting contrast to the rustic fencing and kitchen-garden planting of the potager beyond. Although the change of mood is apparent, the trees are evidence that although the potager may be less formal, it will still be orderly.

right The geometry created by the three stone balls in this Irish garden is gloriously undermined by the untrimmed nature of the copper beech hedge, resulting in a pleasing balance of formality and informality.

Paths within the garden need a destination. This may sound obvious, but it is not unusual to visit gardens where a path does nothing more than lead from the house to the fence at the end of the property. It may have access points to different parts of the garden along its way, but the lack of an arrival point can be disappointing. This is readily remedied by placing an object at the end of the path—a focal point, either modest or grand—which will draw you toward it. A beautifully planted pot, a seat to sit on and admire the view, a statue, or a water feature all have the power to lure you to the farthest end of the garden.

Perspective is an important element in this type of garden, and there are tricks that can emphasize this effect and make a space seem larger than it actually is. A central path that tapers as it recedes toward the end of the garden will mislead the eye into thinking that the plot is longer than it really is, an effect that can be enhanced by gradually reducing the size of any pots flanking the path.

far left Flanked with topiary boxwood balls, an antique bench is given added importance within the garden. The bench has been painted a strong shade of blue, which allows its delicate pattern to stand out against the background of foliage and echo the color of the paving stones.

left Pairs of terracotta pots planted with white daisies stand on plinths on each side of a central path. Surrounded by a clipped boxwood hedge, the pots of flowers draw the eye to the ultimate destination— the pretty white bench at the end of the path.

right There is a pleasing symmetry in this tableau. A clipped tree stands like a green parasol over a pair of painted wooden chairs and terracotta pots planted with boxwood balls.

above **There is a satisfying balance to the curve of this informal hedge, echoed by the gravel path and the clean-cut edge to the lawn.**

left **A curving path leads sinuously toward a half-concealed tower at the end of the garden. Low-growing bamboo lines the left-hand side of the path, while on the other side a line of large stones draws you to your destination.**

Topiary is very much at home in the formal garden—it helps emphasize symmetry far more effectively than less structured plants. Where space is restricted, topiary looks best when it is limited to no more than two different shapes, and it should always be placed in mirrored pairs or it will unsettle the atmosphere in the garden. In a large garden you have more freedom—provided the layout is strictly symmetrical, some variation in shapes can introduce a lighter mood.

Not everyone responds positively to the formal rigidity of a symmetrical garden, even if it is softened by planting. If it all seems too ordered for your taste, you may feel more at home if your peaceful garden is a place of balance rather than symmetry. Here gentle curves define shape and contemporary materials challenge the old order, creating something new, yet still evoking a sense of restfulness in a 21st-century garden.

Although there are exceptions, the balanced garden is generally less structured than its symmetrical counterpart, with its architectural elements placed among informal plantings. There are fewer obvious guidelines than in the symmetrical garden and consequently more experimentation is called for. This approach is not suitable for anyone who is likely to fret when confronted by uncertainty. The aim is to create a peaceful garden, but if you have sleepless nights as your garden evolves, it is rather self-defeating.

previous page A precise geometry of radiating circles underlies this Impressionistic planting. To achieve such a natural-looking result requires real plant knowledge and careful management, or it could end up looking like a once-formal garden now overtaken by weeds. At the heart of the garden is a circular chamomile lawn.

left This monolithic, minimalist-style garden is not for the faint-hearted or for those who have a penchant for soft planting, but it has an austere beauty. Over the wall, a tree attempts to break in; but within its boundaries, only a small square of grass relieves a courtyard that is more about architecture than horticulture.

You may have a strong, instinctive feeling for colors and shapes that combine harmoniously, and creating a garden in this way can be a delightfully liberating affair. Free of the constraints of rules and fashion, you can shape a garden that is truly yours.

If, however, you are attracted by this style of garden, you may find that it is more difficult to visualize on paper than is a geometric design. Curves are better marked out on the ground; and when it comes to placing objects in the garden, it is best to experiment with different spots until they feel right. If the object itself is too large, heavy, or tall, use something more manageable that is approximately its shape and size. You can do an awful lot with a few stakes and a ball of string, a chair or a stepladder, and some imagination. Half-close your eyes and check the effect of the positioning on the rest of the garden—and remember to check how you feel about what you see as well as what you think.

Too often we discount intuition, but it is a very useful tool. When we look at a work of art and feel uplifted and enriched by it, we don't necessarily understand the principles of proportion or perspective or have a grasp of color theory, but we often have a positive emotional response that is just as valid as a more informed analysis of the canvas. Similarly, you may know nothing about garden design, but have a strong instinct for colors and shapes that combine harmoniously, and creating a garden in this way can be a delightfully liberating affair. Free of the constraints of rules and fashion, you can shape a garden that is truly yours.

This is not to suggest that balance is unconstrained—far from it, think of traditional scales where all the weight starts off on one side—but the constraints are of your own devising, rather than externally imposed, and how you achieve the balance you seek is a matter of personal judgment. If this all sounds rather esoteric, it isn't. If you feel happy in your garden and there is nothing you want to change, then trust that feeling. You already have your peaceful space, regardless of the dictates of fashion or the opinions of others.

Whether your goal is a garden of balance or symmetry, you should consider its relationship with the architecture of your home and its surroundings. You may have your heart set on a wildflower garden with untrimmed mixed hedging, long grass, and no visibly cultivated areas; but if the setting is a suburban street, it may look more neglected than wild, causing resentment among your neighbors—and your peaceful garden will become a bone of contention rather than a place of sanctuary as intended. Similarly, a modernist house needs a garden that is sympathetic to its architecture, rather than a recreation of some earlier gardening style, or the two will rub up against one another in an uncomfortable manner. The wider view is always an important consideration.

right **Clipped squares of boxwood give this rural garden designed by Tania Compton a formal symmetry that is made more relaxed by their planting with a mixture of roses and herbaceous perennials. In the summer, flowers spill over the hedges, disguising the geometry, which is more evident during the winter months.**

contemplation and relaxation

As you plan your peaceful garden, it is important to remember that it is as much about how the garden is used as about how it looks—a balancing of form and function. Ideally, it should be multifunctional, with open areas for family activities and entertaining, as well as quiet places and hidden corners that are conducive to private contemplation.

The moods conjured up by the words contemplation and relaxation are quite different. There is a weight and seriousness, sometimes even a spiritual dimension, to contemplation, which is generally thought of as a solitary activity, while relaxation is more about physical repose or socializing. To accommodate both within the same garden requires an awareness of these differences.

There is a long history of great or profound thoughts taking place in a garden, from the dawning self-awareness of Adam and Eve as they contemplated their nakedness in the Garden of Eden to Isaac Newton's formulation of the theory of gravity after he was struck on the head by a falling apple. While most of us are unlikely to change the course of history or increase scientific knowledge when we are lost in thought in the garden, we can take inspiration from historic gardens and incorporate into our own some of the elements that have long been believed to aid contemplation.

Zen, Persian, and monastic gardens all explored the meaning of life in different ways. Zen emphasizes meditation and contemplation as ways to achieve self-knowledge, and its highly symbolic gardens represent the pathway to enlightenment. The symmetry, order, and symbolism of a Persian garden are an earthly representation of paradise.

above **It is easy to understand why Monet was so drawn to scenes like this—the floating flowers, the reflections, and the wildlife a pond attracts all invite you to linger, observe, or just relax.**

right **A vine-covered arbor shades a stone terrace where a table and chairs hold promise of alfresco meals with friends and family. At dusk, lanterns light the scene, and the garden is the perfect place to be on a summer evening.**

The very word "paradise" has its origins in Persia, where the word *pardeiza* means an enclosed area. Water was the central, essential element in these gardens; it ensured fertility and cooled the air, but above all it was a metaphor for looking into the soul—as the pools of water mirrored one's image, so the garden was a place for spiritual reflection. During the Middle Ages the cloister gardens of the monastic orders were generally unadorned areas of grass, free from distraction for those who moved in prayer around their perimeters. The physic or infirmary gardens, in which the European monks grew healing plants, far left With the addition of a comfortable chair, this beautiful classical stone portico and its topiary sentinels overlooking a formal pond would make the perfect place to read a novel and dream.

left A wooden dock allows close examination of a pond and its teeming life. Both practical and pleasurable, it makes the pond easier to look after and more accessible. Remove your shoes and sit on its edge, dabbling your feet in the water for a perfect moment of relaxation.

below left A gazebo should always be well removed from the house —a place to go to and get away from the rest of the family, to share a secret, or to enjoy in solitude.

right Water is the great life-giver for all living things, and contemplating it is thought-provoking and relaxing. A wildlife pond like this within a garden is beneficial for you and the environment.

above **This charming gazebo is a home away from home with its pretty paintwork, mixture of furniture, and potted plants on the windowsills. Its appearance belies its origins as a tool shed.**

below **A length of wood tied to a rope and hung from a tree makes a simple swing—an invitation to both children and adults to stop and play.**

opposite **A Georgian-style metal bench is an appropriate choice for a town garden. Underplanted and surrounded by lavender, with a scented climbing rose on the wall behind it and linden trees on each side to create a private corner, this is the perfect spot to read a book in the sunshine or relax with a cold drink in the evening.**

were places where they could contemplate their mortality as they cultivated cures to alleviate the suffering of the sick and the poor. At one end of the abbey there was often a semi-circular garden called a paradise, which supplied flowers to decorate altars and chapels.

Each contains elements that you may like to include in your own garden. The symbolic shapes and materials used in a Zen garden would be appropriate in a contemporary urban environment; the rills and reflecting pools of a Persian garden are ideal for a formal setting, while the healing herbs of a physic garden will fit in well to a country garden. In each case they will help set the mood and aid quiet thoughts.

Relaxation is less demanding—it can be found in a deckchair, on a hammock slung between two trees, lying on the grass looking up at the sky, or in the company of friends sitting around a table. Anywhere, in fact, you feel comfortable enough to forget your day-to-day worries and have a bit of time off.

With a little thought, the same spot can be an aid to both contemplation and relaxation.

above **This rooftop terrace uses a screen of elaeagnus for privacy and as a windbreak, but it is not allowed to grow tall enough to obscure the view, which has its own urban charm, especially at night when buildings are illuminated.**

left **A desk with a perfect view—cool, uncluttered, conducive to thought, the scene provides relief from work but is not full of distraction. Working at home makes it all too easy to be diverted from the matter at hand.**

Anyone who has walked around their own garden at dawn will know that the atmosphere is quite different from other times of day—so different that sometimes it is hard to believe that you are in the same garden. It becomes a place of mystery in the early half-light, with creatures around that you will not see later. If you have never experienced this, it is worth making the effort—you will see the garden in a fresh light (literally) and have a sense of just how peaceful it can be.

In the same way that a garden looks different at different times of day, you can create areas that are used in a variety of ways throughout the day. A quiet moment of contemplation can be experienced standing next to a pond watching the reflections of the clouds pass across its surface, while later, it is the perfect spot in which to relax with a book. A gazebo or deck at the end of the garden can be a foreign land for adventurous children, a relaxing place for a companionable tea party in the afternoon, and an escape from the hurly-burly of family life in the evening. This type of building, whether it is a gazebo or shed, deck or den, should be situated far enough away from the house to make sure it fulfills its function as a refuge.

Try to find room for a swing. Remember when you were a child how you used to go and sit on the swing when you had something to think about? It works just as well when you are an adult.

Too close, and you will be tempted back into domesticity, or it will become an annex of the house with everyone congregating there just when you try to snatch a quiet moment.

In the center of old Amsterdam in Holland, all the 17th-century houses that line the canals of the Grachtengordel have garden houses at the farthest point from the house. Some are grand stone affairs with intricate carvings and marble floors; others are built from wood with decorative fretwork embellishments, while elsewhere the tradition continues with modern buildings beyond the flower-filled gardens. The uses of the buildings are as varied as the styles of their architecture, but what they have in common is that they are removed from the influence of domestic life and as such can be used as places of refuge.

Treehouses have traditionally been children's territory, but increasingly adults are having them built for themselves. Very different from the dens fashioned from old planks and crates that I remember from my childhood, some are proper rooms perched in trees like the Swiss Family

Robinson's treetop aerie, with chairs and tables, beds, and even electricity and running water in some instances. Others restrict themselves to being lofty lookouts, but either way, they offer a perfect opportunity to relax and recapture the excitement of childhood adventures.

So, too, do swings and hammocks; after all relaxation is as much about fun as it is about rest, so even if children don't regularly use your garden, try to find room for a swing—not a modern playground swing, but something old-fashioned to hang from a tree. Visiting children will be delighted, and it is guaranteed to be well used by adults, too. Remember when you were a child how you used to go and sit on the swing when you had something to think about? It works just as well when you are an adult. Hammocks are a source of entertainment as well as ultimate relaxation. The entertainment is to be had from watching others trying to get into the hammock without falling out; sitting up in a hammock is neither easy nor recommended. The relaxation comes when they succeed. Sling a hammock in a secluded corner of the garden where you will be left undisturbed.

Finding peace and quiet in the city is a far harder prospect, but rooftop gardens, balconies, and terraces do lift you above the hustle and bustle and provide an outside space for those who spend most of their lives indoors. The ideal arrangement in this type of raised urban garden is a low screen of planting that gives shelter and privacy when you are sitting down but does not obscure the view. In the

contemplation and relaxation **53**

right **A simple wooden bench tucked away in the corner of this building offers privacy, concealment, or shelter from the rain.**

far right **A suitably rustic chair and table blend in perfectly in this woodland clearing. Made from robust materials, they can be left out all year round so that they are always available for an impulse visit.**

absence of countryside, this sense of space is a valuable commodity and becomes a beautiful sight when lit at night.

An old-fashioned veranda or a terrace next to the house may provide the occasional quiet moment for contemplation early in the morning or in the evening, but its primary function is as an informal gathering place. It is usually positioned to make the best of the climate. Sheltered, sometimes shady and certainly convenient, it is where family and friends get together for alfresco

meals, to exchange confidences, or enjoy a siesta in a comfy chair. Pots of favorite plants often find a home here, and tending them, especially if they are sweetly scented, is a relaxing pastime for those who find it hard to sit down for long.

A garden that is used for contemplation and relaxation needs plenty of places to sit. These include solitary chairs in secluded corners where you can think deep thoughts, benches in sunny spots surrounded by scented plants where you can exchange

left These days, treehouses are as likely to be built for adults as for children. Either way, they are a perfect place to get another perspective on the garden—or even life! Before you build, you should check with your neighbors if it overlooks their yard, and in some areas a building permit may be needed.

opposite above Removable covers and synthetic fillings are best for outdoor cushions. If they are left out overnight, they can be washed and dried without permanent damage.

opposite below A quiet bench well away from the house is a refuge from interruptions, ringing telephones, and all the other demands of life. It's a place to think, to dream, or catch up on your reading (although a cushion or two might be advisable).

confidences or sit in companionable silence, and folding chairs that can be easily moved to take advantage of a patch of sun or shade, depending on the season. Seats carefully positioned around the garden will reveal the best views to visitors, or encourage them to pause alongside a pond or other garden feature that is worthy of closer examination. Comfortably cushioned chairs in a gazebo might persuade you to take shelter there instead of retreating indoors during summer showers—there is something delightfully frivolous about sitting somewhere like this waiting for the rain to stop instead of rushing inside.

Eating outdoors is one of life's great pleasures, provided it is a comfortable experience. Ideally the table and chairs should be close to the kitchen—that way, it's easy to be spontaneous and decide on the spur of the moment to decamp outside. The idea of eating at the far end of the garden may appeal, but the reality is that someone has to carry everything there and back, a chore that is not always conducive

to domestic harmony. Have an occasional picnic there instead, and leave the table and chairs somewhere more convenient.

Because it needs to withstand the weather, most garden furniture is a compromise between comfort and durability, which means that a good supply of cushions is essential. Keep a large basket of them on the porch, or in the gazebo or shed, so they are easy to bring out and put away. Make sure they are washable, and if you live somewhere where the winters are cold or damp, bring the cushions indoors and store them in a warm place or they will become musty. Small details like these may seem trifling, but when they are a cause of irritation or argument, they can interfere with the peaceful atmosphere of the garden.

special places

Within every garden there are places that are invested with
meaning, places where an object, a plant, or a view has particular
significance for the gardener. It can be a memento recalling love
or loss, a work of art, or a even a tree grown from a seed.

What makes a place special? It is your
relationship with that place and how
that connection was forged. Maybe it
brought you comfort in adversity, calm
when all around was in turmoil, or joy in
a troubled world. But it need not be the
big experiences of life that make this
link; sometimes it is the private pleasures:
finding the first snowdrop in midwinter,
watching a fledgling fly, or picking and
tasting the first peas you have ever
grown—simple things that can tie you to
a particular spot in the garden. When
life gets complicated, you can go to that

right A door left ajar is an invitation to explore further. There is always a sense of excitement and anticipation about what might lie beyond.

opposite left A spiral of stones gathered from within this English garden and laid on the moss-covered ground draws you in to its heart. Through the year this space retains its special quality—cool refuge in summer, intriguing land art in winter.

opposite right A modern garden undergoes a change of mood when it is briefly transformed by a carpet of pink cherry-blossom petals.

special spot, or visit it in your imagination and feel comforted.

A special space can be something private and exclusive to you or a shared experience. When it is shared, it can be a way of communicating to others how you feel about them or your garden, but be discriminating about who you choose to do this with or you may risk spoiling the place or the relationship.

It may be that your special space needs no embellishment, but sometimes it is nice to celebrate the relationship by adding your own decorative touches to an otherwise low-key spot. "Found" objects gathered from around the garden often work best; they have an integrity and a rightness that can be missing from imported materials. This type of decoration is reminiscent of the cave paintings, dolmens, and menhirs of our earliest ancestors.

On the other hand, a work of art by a favorite artist may find a perfect left A mirrored archway creates the illusion of another garden—the ultimate special space—visible but not attainable. Angling the mirror so it is not approached straight helps sustain the illusion. Keep it clean though, or it will fool no one.

below The beauty and dignity of a sculpture of this quality will never pall. A treasured memento of travel to a faraway place, it also acts as a reminder of happy times. Such a fine work of art is a very special addition to a garden and needs to be carefully positioned.

61

home in your special place. It can be fitting to mark an unexpected windfall or work well done with this type of memorial. Make sure whatever you add has some significance, or it will be little more than furniture—filling the space but adding nothing to its meaning. Works of art, when appropriate, give structure to a place and act as anchor points that focus the attention. Over time their beauty changes and transforms as they become weathered and they settle into their surroundings.

If works of art are beyond your means or do not appeal, there are several less costly alternatives worth considering. Salvage yards are filled with all manner of extraordinary items in all sorts of materials, from broken columns to old metalwork, which can add character and a

sense of history to your garden. Sometimes a stroll around one of them will present you with the perfect object at a great price.

Mirrors can be used to create the illusion of a larger space or another garden through an arch or doorway, especially if the mirror is slightly angled so that visitors do not see their reflections as they approach it. Mirrors also bring light to otherwise dark areas; similarly, stained-glass panels positioned so the sun can shine through the jeweled colors will transform a space into something utterly magical.

One of the most seductive features in a garden is a door in a wall. It harks back to childhood and the world of the imagination conjured up by books like *The Secret Garden* by Frances Hodgson Burnett and the Narnia stories

Works of art give structure to a place and act as anchor points that focus the attention. Over time their beauty changes and transforms as they become weathered and settle into their surroundings.

opposite left **Garden art does not need to be priceless to be effective. This wind chime was made by suspending flattened spoons and an old bell from fishing line.**

opposite right **Designer Ivan Hicks created a woodland work of art by piling a cairn of stones on top of a reclaimed stone frame.**

right **A magnificent urn fashioned from slate by sculptor Joe Smith is an object of wonder as well as something of great beauty. It needs no embellishment, and the surrounding planting has rightly been kept at a low level.**

far left An arching pair of rustic poles marks the beginning of a grassy path winding through a wildflower meadow and perfectly frames the distant tree, which might otherwise go unremarked.

left The rustic poles at the edge of the meadow echo the shape of the archway that leads from the garden, drawing you forward to explore what lies beyond.

by C. S. Lewis. Some years ago, I was lost in the depths of the Somerset countryside; arriving at the outskirts of an unknown village, I stopped next to a wall to get my bearings. Looking up from my map, I noticed a door in the wall that bore the simple legend "To the Garden." Feeling like a character from *Alice in Wonderland*, I felt compelled to investigate, excited yet also a touch fearful of what I might find beyond. I'm pleased to report that I neither fell down a well nor encountered the Red Queen. Instead, I found myself in the garden that had once belonged to the great English plantswoman, Margery Fish—a memorable visit that has forged a special relationship between me and that place.

Simple touches are often more effective than grand decorative flourishes. When framing a view, it is the view, not the frame, that should draw the attention. The frame provides an appropriate setting, but if it is unnecessarily elaborate, it will act as a distraction. Subtlety deepens the experience. A curving path that leads you on to an unseen destination, a half-hidden gate in a hedge, a door left ajar in a wall—all invite exploration, and the pleasure and surprise at the discovery of a wonderful view or a hidden garden is all the greater for the journey that has been taken. A sense of mystery enlivens a garden and promises revelation.

Plants, too, make a vital contribution to a special space. They can be used to enclose, conceal, frame, left At the end of this path a quirky, homemade fence and arch give the farthest part of the garden a sense of enclosure without totally concealing the space from the rest of the garden. A solid fence would make the garden feel smaller.

opposite A grass pathway, its margins softened by plants, leads to a wooden doorway, tempting you to explore farther. Even if the door does not conceal a hidden garden, by its very existence it makes the space seem bigger.

or surround your chosen spot. Their colors, textures, and fragrances help define and emphasize the mood. A shady garden can be enlivened by drifts of white flowers that bring light and contrast—a wooded glade becomes romantic when softly illuminated by white foxgloves and martagon lilies. A sunny corner, where fragrant lavender and rosemary surround a stone seat and creeping thymes grow among the flagstones, will be filled with color and a heady fragrance. Climbing plants that are allowed to clothe a wall and curtain an archway offer both concealment and discovery. Sometimes a single plant is all you need, especially in a contemporary minimalist garden—a rustling bamboo that moves gently in the wind, an architectural plant that throws dramatic shadows on a painted wall, a solitary tree to soften the stones that surround it. The right plant in the right place.

Sometimes it is the plants themselves that make the space special—it might be a rose grown from a cutting from your childhood garden, a souvenir of a lovely vacation, or a tree raised from a seed by one of your children who has now grown up and left home. Plants like this are loaded with significance and create a living bond between you and your garden.

My own garden is full of such plants, and when I walk around it, I find myself reliving the experiences and thinking of friends and family. There is the olive tree I bought back from Tuscany as a sapling, now ten feet tall; a blue perennial cornflower known by all the family as "Mrs. Bottomley" in honor of the person who gave us the first small plant from her garden, and most significantly for me, a perfect, richly scented pink rose, reputedly grown from a cutting taken from a rose that grew on the poet Omar Khayyam's grave. I planted it originally in the garden of the first home I lived in as an adult, and when I moved, it was potted up and moved with me. It then spent twenty years in that pot moving from place to place, and it is only now that I have at last found my special space that I feel ready once more to plant it in my garden.

opposite An old stone column hints at the possibility of an earlier, more formal garden, lost long ago. The trimmed topiary counterpoints the air of abandon, showing that the effect is intentional.

above left A doorway in a wall is the most romantic of entrances to a garden.

below left A beautifully simple wooden bench carved with a couple's initials transforms this wooded glade into a trysting place.

special places **69**

tranquillity for the senses

soothing colors

soothing textures

light and shade

Detail is as important in the peaceful garden as design and layout. Choosing the right colors and textures, and observing the effect of light and shade help set the mood. Let your emotions be your guide—if a color, a texture, or a play of light calms and pleases you, it will contribute to the overall effect of the garden.

soothing colors

The peaceful garden requires a subtle and restrained palette, where plants blend in harmonious drifts. Cool, soft, or pastel colors will complement the calm mood.

The gentle, soothing presence of green is at the core of the peaceful garden. The myriad shades of the foliage form the backdrop and supply the supporting cast for the flowers, their delicate beauty becoming all the more apparent when set in a sea of green. It is a constantly metamorphosing color, from the fresh acid greens of spring through the dusty greens of summer to the transformations of autumn and the rich, glossy leaves of evergreens and glaucous hues of conifers in winter. In his poem "The Garden," the poet Andrew Marvell (1621–1678) wrote of "a green thought in a green shade." Nearly four hundred years later, we still feel the pull of that phrase, and like

Marvell will often seek out a cool, bosky corner of the garden in which to think quiet thoughts.

In the peaceful flower garden, too, green often predominates, while the other colors which feature are chosen to be complementary rather than contrasting. Whites, creams, pinks, blues, and purples all blend together harmoniously, and soft yellows have their place as well, but contrasting colors such as oranges, bright reds, and bright yellows should be avoided; they intensify the greens and make the effect less calming. A garden with little or no foliage, or one where foliage is secondary to the flowers, may have impact, but it is seldom peaceful in its mood. Think of the bulb fields of Holland, where

above **The starburst flower heads of alliums last many weeks in the garden, and the seedheads that follow are just as decorative, if not quite so colorful.**

left **In early spring it is unusual to see pink flowers; the blooms of this alpine clematis (*Clematis macropetala*) are an exception.**

opposite **At the foot of a hedge, the long grass is left untrimmed to let the alliums and Queen Anne's lace bloom undisturbed. The color of the alliums is just a shade darker than the flowers on the Judas tree (*Cercis siliquastrum*).**

right The intense blue of morning glory is one of the most appealing colors in the garden, and the transience of the flower adds to its beauty.

below As flowers develop from bud to fully opened flower, their colors change; the cerise of this unfurling allium will soften with age.

opposite The flowering habit of the colorful and unusual *Primula vialii* resembles that of a wild orchid with its succession of tiny flowers opening over many weeks. The rust-colored cone at the top of the flower head conceals the unopened buds.

great gashes of color transect the landscape, or carpet bedding plantings with their hectic patterns—both attract attention, but neither soothes the eye.

If this all sounds rather too wishy-washy for your taste, don't despair. Although the palette may be restricted, the range of shades is not, and there is plenty of opportunity to use rich colors. Combining deep shades of purple and pink with strong blues creates an intensely colorful tapestry, and softer plantings always look more interesting when some dark tones are included.

Interweaving the plants blends the colors like an Impressionist painter. This is most easily done by planting in irregular-shaped drifts of uneven numbers of plants. This effect can work well even in a formal garden. Boxwood edging or other features provide the structure and

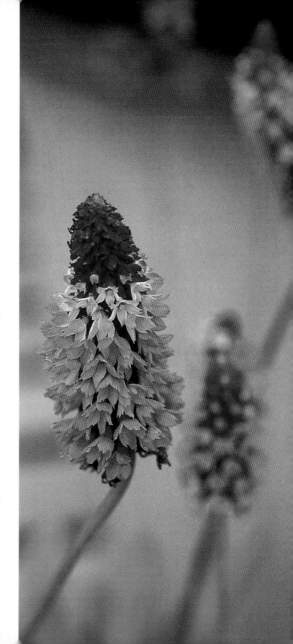

PICTURES OVERLEAF
above left **Although not quite as vigorous as its green cousin, the rich, dark coloring of purple basil makes it worth growing.**

below left **The canna lily is a tender plant, but nurture it for the striking colors of its architectural leaves and its bright flower spikes.**

center **The steely blue flowers of** *Eryngium bourgatii* **have an appealing thistlelike quality. In the evening light, their color appears to deepen.**

right **Walking along this grassy path, lined with the soft colors and heady fragrance of the marjoram** (*Origanum*), **lavender cotton** (*Santolina*), **and catnip** (*Nepeta*), **is guaranteed to be a sensory pleasure.**

above far left *Ammi majus* is a delicate, cultivated form of Queen Anne's lace usually grown as a hardy annual.

above center The shades of *Astrantia major* range from white to pink and red. Grow in light shade where the paler colors show up well.

above left The foxglove *Digitalis purpurea* f. *albiflora* is a stately presence in a bed or a woodland garden.

below far left These white agapanthus make excellent container plants in full sun.

below center White flag iris flower briefly but beautifully.

below left Flowering grasses such as *Eriophorum angustifolium* have a subtle beauty.

FLOWERS FOR SOOTHING COLORS

Agapanthus

Allium

Ammi majus (bishop's flower)

Astrantia major (masterwort)

Cerinthe

Clematis macropetala (alpine clematis)

Digitalis purpurea f. *albiflora* (white foxglove)

Eryngium bourgatii (sea holly)

Helleborus orientalis (hellebore)

Hesperis matronalis (sweet rocket)

Hydrangea

Ipomoea (morning glory)

Iris

Lavandula (lavender)

Nepeta (catnip)

Nigella (love-in-a-mist)

Origanum (marjoram)

Papaver somniferum (opium poppy)

definition for the soft planting within. Such planting, however, is not suited to a symmetrical arrangement and can easily look messy, especially if a plant or two fails and leaves the whole display looking somewhat gap-toothed.

Color-themed gardens are popular and can be very restful. Sissinghurst's White Garden is a good example—with its white, silver, and gray plants, it is a serene and inspiring place to sit. Even though the palette is restricted, there is an enormous variety of subtly different colors that blend together to create the overall picture.

Depending on the time of day, colors can look very different—blues and whites tend to look harsh or washed out at midday, yet at dawn and dusk they take on a luminous quality that is hypnotic in its effect. This type of transformation is at the heart of the peaceful garden.

far left A green-painted bench echoes the color of the surrounding foliage and the grass beneath it. This subtle coloration is ideal in a peaceful garden.

left Ferns such as this *Dryopteris dilatata* are perfect plants for a shady woodland garden.

below A leafy path edged with hedges and overhung by trees draws you deeper and deeper into the garden. There is no need for any color except green in this type of setting.

right The brilliant green of young ostrich fern (*Matteuccia struthiopteris*) fronds unfold in a consummate display of natural beauty.

soothing textures

Every plant and every surface within the garden has a texture and a relationship with its surroundings. Soothing textures are more about that relationship than the feel of a leaf or the finish of a stone.

An easy way to understand the relationship between different textures is to look at a Zen garden. Its timeless and peaceful beauty is an enduring legacy of the Buddhist monks who created it. By creating symbolic gardens that represented the pathway to enlightenment, the monks were able to explain the principles of Zen to their followers.

Each rock, tree, or shrub is placed with infinite care and has special meaning. A rock placed horizontally can represent the sky, vertically the earth, or depending on shape or position, it may be an island or even an animal. A clipped shrub symbolizes billowing clouds, and the use and form of small pebbles, gravel, and sand help create an atmosphere conducive to meditation.

above **The gentle curve and smooth finish of the wooden deck contrast pleasingly with the varied textures of the rough slate and mixed stones. A carpet of cherry blossom petals adds a temporary softness to the composition.**

above left **There is a pleasing juxtaposition of materials and textures in this picture—a wooden deck gives way to concrete steps and a low wall that leads onto concrete stepping stones. The hard surfaces are made less brutal by the rounded stones that surround them, and a grassy plant softens the setting even more.**

above right **The smooth textures and linear design of the etched glass window and plain paneled walls are emphasized by decking, laid at right angles to the building. Everything changes when deck meets stones.**

below **Sometimes all you need to highlight texture is a variation in size.**

Each element is pared-down, simple and refined. Change is not necessary. There is nothing superfluous or frivolous, no giving way to the temptation to include a favorite flower or put a seat in a sunny corner. In the Zen garden, everything has added meaning, and looking at it can be a profound experience.

This doesn't mean that every peaceful garden should follow the Zen model, but it can help you to reach an understanding of how to combine elements successfully when you mix

left **Very much an outdoor room, this garden has been furnished and decorated with contrasting textures —a carpet of gravel, differing surfaces on the painted walls, concrete sofas with matting cushions, and a bamboo table. The tree in the corner is the only living thing in this garden.**

PLANTS FOR SOOTHING TEXTURES

Artemisia 'Powis Castle'—ferny foliage

Ballota pseudodictamnus—wooly foliage

Bamboos—ferny foliage

Eryngium alpinum—tickly/prickly, ferny leaves

Eschscholzia (California poppy)—silky petals and ferny foliage and flowers

Ferns—curling fronds

Foeniculum vulgare (fennel)—ferny foliage

Hosta—bold, ribbed leaves

Papaver somniferum (opium poppy)—silky flowers and ferny foliage

Pelargonium tomentosum—hairy, ferny foliage

Romneya coulteri (matilja poppy)—papery flowers and ferny foliage

Salix caprea (pussy willow)—velvety catkins and bold foliage

Salvia officinalis (sage)—bold, rough leaves

Sedum—bold, fleshy leaves

Stachys byzantina—bold, wooly leaves

Stipa tenuifolia—hairy

Thalictrum—ferny foliage

Verbascum olympicum (Olympic mullein)—bold, wooly leaves and flower spikes

planting and hard landscaping. Once more, this is an aspect of garden design that needs to involve your emotional response. If the juxtaposition of two different textures feels right, then it usually is; if, on the other hand, you feel uncomfortable, maybe you need to try some other solutions.

The obvious way to check how you react to textures is to touch them. Hold a smooth stone in your hand and notice how you turn it round and round; pick up a handful of gravel and pour it from one hand to the other; run some sand through your fingers—these are tactile experiences and will help you understand how you relate to the materials. Not all

soothing textures **85**

responses are positive; some people hate sand (it reminds them of gritty sandwiches on the beach), while others dislike gravel surfaces because they love to walk barefoot in the grass. By exploring your responses to the different textures before you embark on your garden, you can create an environment tailored to your own preferences.

But the peaceful garden does not consist solely of rounded stones and velvety leaves. It is the relationship of one thing to another that is important, and here a contrast often works better than textures or shapes that are too similar. Think of a bed where all the plants have similar leaves, or a garden where every

surface is the same—the effect is more likely to be boring than soothing.

There are words which describe texture or shape that have the power to soothe—words like round, curved, smooth, undulating. They can be used as guides to some of the textures to include in your garden, especially the surfaces —paving, steps, walls, and water features. The materials that are used for these elements in the garden are most successful when they are sympathetic to their surroundings. Polished concrete, slate, and metal are perfectly at home in an urban setting, while rustic wood, weathered brick, and stone blend seamlessly in a country garden. This sensitivity to the surroundings is part of what makes a garden peaceful—jarring notes should be avoided. Imagine a country garden where a blue glass mulch has been spread on a bed, or a city garden where a cottage garden arch, complete with roses, is placed in minimalist surroundings. Eccentric maybe, but definitely not soothing.

The materials traditionally used for building in your area can also be used as a guide. If houses are built of granite, a garden that features sandstone will look out of place—think of the two materials alongside one another, and it will give you an idea of whether your choice is appropriate. In this instance, slate looks much better with granite than sandstone. When the material is right, its texture becomes less significant. And once the hard landscaping has been resolved, it becomes much easier to choose suitable plants.

There are as many plant textures as there are plants; the differences, sometimes obvious, left This pared-down urban terrace where textures dominate and plants take a back seat requires no more than a couple of hours of maintenance a year. A simple square trellis encloses the area, and the few plants that grow against it focus the eye inside the garden. Irregular-shaped blocks of stone are set in smooth pebbles. The terrace is edged with concrete, which has a sunken recess for a barbecue or fire.

right There is a monumental feeling to this stone wall with its rough-hewn surfaces. Built solely as a blockwork wall, it would feel imprisoning, but intersected by the pillars of stone it becomes far more significant. Any plants would detract from its power, and the simple grass carpet seems entirely appropriate.

sometimes subtle, are as important as the variation of color within a garden. Read through a list of plant descriptions, and texture is a key element, whether soft and hairy, plump and fleshy, deeply ridged, prickly, fuzzy, or thorny. You will respond to the texture as much as you do to the other details.

When you walk around the garden, notice how often your hand reaches out to touch a flower, stroke a leaf, or feel the smoothness of bark. Your brain may not always register what you are doing, but in the same way that stroking a pet induces calm, this tactile tour of the garden is a soothing experience. In most gardens the plant textures are incidental, but when you are making a peaceful garden, you can consciously select your favorite surfaces, barks, or patinas. They will sustain the garden long after flowers have faded. In the same way that the blending of colors creates patterns in the garden, so the combining and blending of textures gives rhythm and variation to the planting.

Viewed from a distance, texture is about shape and outline—after all, touch cannot be experienced from afar. But interesting outlines and contrasting shapes will draw you closer until you are near enough for a truly tactile experience. This is where far left **Bluestone and pink bricks compose this small, square, textured terrace, leading to a graveled area.**

left **An informal path has steps made from salvaged railroad ties and gravel. Plants grow happily in the gravel, softening the edges and self-seeding readily.**

above **The curled tips of hosta leaves push through a seemingly hostile environment of pebbles and stones. At present the hard landscaping is more evident than the plant, but once the hosta leaves are open, they will dominate.**

right **This is a garden full of contrasting textures, not all of which combine happily. A boardwalk leads across a dry garden of bold, linear plants such as palms, grasses, and phormiums. Behind this carefully set scene, a conventional garden intrudes rather uncomfortably.**

above This wall, made from Welsh slate using dry-laid building techniques, is both beautiful and practical. It snakes its way through the garden, dividing different areas, its rough texture a contrast to its curving shape.

right Different hard landscaping materials make an interesting pattern on this garden floor. In the foreground the linear planks, set in stones, draw you deeper into the garden, where the curving setts lead you to either side of the central area laid with simple paving slabs.

above left **Like fragments of lost paving from an ancient ruin, these stones, carefully placed among pebbles, have more presence than conventional paving.**

above right **This patterned path in a herb garden has a wonderful patina of age. Natural materials such as stone, brick, and tile age beautifully and become more subtle as years pass.**

texture becomes really significant. Surfaces—of leaves, stems, bark, fruit, and even flowers—gain their character as much from their texture as their color, and in gardens where color is restricted, texture is essential to avert monotony. Describe a leaf as puckered, ribbed, rough, smooth, shiny, matte, prickly, thorny, or furry, and you quickly realize how very different they are one from another, not just in appearance, but in the effect they have on the general view. Shiny surfaces advance, appearing closer than they actually are, while flat finishes have the opposite effect and tend to recede.

There are three basic shapes of foliage in the garden—bold, linear, and ferny. Bold encompasses the big leaves like *Fatsia*, *Gunnera*, *Rheum*, and *Hosta*; these sorts of leaves are popular in tropical or architectural planting designs. Linear includes swordlike foliage and many of the grasses, while ferny covers the softer shapes, including, of course, ferns. By combining these shapes in your planting, you create instant interest. If you still find it difficult to grasp the impact that texture has on planting, try taking black-and-white photographs of your garden. By removing the distraction of color, texture comes to the fore. If the pictures all look rather monotonous, it is an indication that you need to introduce more contrasting textural effects.

Bold foliage plants bring substance to the garden, but scale and proportion also need to be considered. Including the grandest of these plants in a small garden can leave room for little else—fine if it is a simple, minimalist garden, but very limiting if it is not. Also bear in mind that some plants, such as *Gunnera*, die right down in winter, leaving very little evidence of their otherwise impressive presence. On a smaller scale, hostas provide some of the best bold foliage in the garden. Their large ridged, pleated, or puckered leaves have a wonderful textural quality, and the color variations add further interest. They, too, have their limitations—they are a favorite food of slugs and snails, and their beautiful leaves can be reduced to lace where these pests are a problem. In such cases, hostas are best grown in pots protected by copper tape or another deterrent.

Although not all linear plants are grasses, they make up by far the largest group of plants, encompassing everything grassy from giant bamboos to the prettily compact *Festuca glauca*. Grass, in all its

above left *Stipa gigantea* is the stateliest of grasses. From its base it sends up a spectacular fountain of tall flowering stalks that turn golden bronze during summer.

above center *Briza maxima* is commonly known as quaking grass, a perfect name for this delicate annual with ever-moving pendent seedheads. Their appearance invites you to run your fingers through them.

above right The bronze-red leaves and large clusters of delicate purple flower heads of *Panicum virgatum* 'Shenandoah' make this a particularly appealing grass.

opposite *Stipa tenuissima* is one of the most tactile grasses, with its soft green hairlike foliage tinged bronze at the tips. Its texture is reminiscent of doll's hair. The shape and texture of the grass contrast nicely with the knapweed.

shapes and forms, provides many of the most soothing textures in the garden. And not just the ornamental varieties either—think of your lawn and the pleasure to be gained from walking on it barefoot, or lying on your back looking up at the sky. Both are highly evocative experiences, often sending you back to your childhood and more carefree times. If you haven't done either in a long time, you are missing out on two of the simplest, purest pleasures to be found in the garden.

In recent years ornamental grasses have become increasingly popular with gardeners as informal planting has taken over from the orderly beds of the past. The relaxed, fluid effect of grasses is perfectly at home in contemporary gardens, whether urban or rural. The fact that they are very easy to grow, undemanding, and look wonderful throughout the year has also helped their popularity. Even in the dead of winter, the dry stems and seedheads have a presence in the garden, especially when they are rimed with frost. They are important for wildlife, too—beneficial insects hibernate among the dry foliage, and birds find valuable food in the seedheads. Leaving the grasses untrimmed fits in well with their correct care. They should be cut back, thinned, or divided in spring

opposite **The cat's-tongue roughness of sage leaves does not appeal to everyone.**

this page **Succulent plants beg to be touched. From the smallest to the largest, their fleshy leaves have an irresistible tactile quality. They store** moisture in their foliage so will grow happily in arid conditions such as the tops of gateposts, or in shallow containers on tabletops. With their modest demands they could easily be overlooked, but close study reveals fantastic variations in color and texture.

above **Before young hosta leaves have opened fully, the contrasting color and texture of their undersides is attractively revealed. Noticing these gradual transformations is one of the pleasures of the peaceful garden.**

right **Droplets of water hang on the ferny foliage of a fennel plant. Touching the plant when it is wet is a very different—and not necessarily enjoyable— experience, compared to running your fingers through it when it is dry.**

rather than in the fall. This will prevent rotting, usually caused by water getting into the crown.

The third basic shape—ferny—naturally includes many ferns. Some ferns will grow happily in dry shade or other difficult situations, and their delicate fronds contrast softly with the other, more architectural shapes. In sunny, open sites, other plants with fernlike foliage are more appropriate— *Thalictrum, Artemisia, Eschscholzia,* and *Senecio cineraria* are just a few examples.

It is useful to have lists of plants that fit into the different categories when you are planning your garden. One of the best ways to compile such a list is to visit a good garden center and make a note of anything that appeals to you under the three

Hostas provide some of the best bold foliage in the garden. Their large ridged, pleated, or puckered leaves have a wonderful texture.

headings bold, linear, and ferny. Not only will this broaden your plant knowledge, but you will also have a clearer understanding of the different shapes, which are just as relevant whether you are looking at a tiny alpine or a 15-foot-tall bamboo.

As you make your choices, other categories and sub-categories will also become evident, and this is where texture really comes into play. Wooly-leaved plants like *Stachys byzantina*, also known as lamb's-ears, are irresistible—their leaves recall a favorite stuffed toy from childhood—while the Olympic mullein, *Verbascum olympicum*, has huge, bold, wooly leaves and flower spikes that bear golden flowers. While you are making your list, notice the plants that you touch and include them, too. Roses may be prickly, but their flower petals feel like silk. Sedums are usually bought for their bright fall flowers and their ability to attract butterflies, but their cool, fleshy leaves are good to touch. Fennel is thought of as a culinary herb, but its ferny foliage looks wonderful in the flowerbed, too, and brushing against it is pleasantly tickly. The textures in a peaceful garden are as much about the tactile experience as they are about their appearance.

left **The delicate unfurling leaves of the aptly named hart's-tongue fern, *Asplenium scolopendrium*, do not have the usual ferny foliage of the genus. Their shiny, rather leathery leaves have a strong linear quality.**

light and shade

The interplay of light and shade brings life to the garden and influences its mood. Light changes constantly during the day, sometimes subtly and sometimes dramatically. Without this variation, the garden would be a less intriguing place and much of its magic would be lost.

Our eyes continually adjust to light, which means that we are not always aware of how altered a view or even a solitary flower can look in differing light conditions. In the peaceful garden, it is helpful to observe these changes; it is a pleasant activity, and the understanding you gain may lead you to make alterations or improvements to your outside space. Watch how light filters through plants onto the ground below, creating shadow patterns; lie on your back under a tree and see how sunlight illuminates the leaves; or sit next to a pond and notice the play of light on water. If you have never consciously noticed these things before, it will be a revelation. Use a camera as an impartial observer—photographs taken of the same scene throughout the day will reveal just how much the differing light affects the results.

As the sun moves across the garden, the quality of light undergoes many transformations. At dawn the light is soft and diffuse, starting quite cold and gray, and warming as the sun rises. This is the favorite time of day for professional garden photographers—plants are fresh and often dew-laden, and there are no strong contrasts or shadows. By noon, with the sun at its highest point, the garden is full of light and shade. In direct light, only strongly colored plants can stand the competition; others tend to look bleached. Shady areas lack definition, and here it is the pale colors that stand out from the crowd. With the approach of evening, shadows lengthen, and the light softens once more, bathing the garden in a golden glow before fading to darkness.

The time of year and weather conditions also affect the quality of light. Even on a cloudy day, left **Attractive glass lanterns** are suspended at different levels from the branch of a tree, softly illuminating their surroundings. In the absence of specially designed glass lanterns, ordinary jelly jars containing candles or votives can be hung from wires to create a similar effect.

right **By twining pinprick lights** through a dark-leaved violet, the coloring and droplets of moisture are brought into focus.

far right **Torches are a** wonderful way to light a garden on a special occasion. Pushed in among plants, they can mark a path or simply act as decorations. Don't place them too close to path edges where clothing might catch fire.

Arranging your garden so that it makes the best possible use of any natural light will make it a more welcoming place.

there are variations—with thick cloud cover, the garden appears flat and one-dimensional, but as the cloud thins, shafts of light or dappling bring it back to life. In hot weather or where pollution is a problem, the light is often hazy, while in sunny winter weather or after rain, it can be crystal clear.

We cannot control the seasons or the weather, but light and shade can make a positive contribution to the garden. In the same way that artificial lighting varies in a room—bright light for general use and soft light for intimate corners—arranging your garden so that it makes the best possible use of any natural light will make it a more welcoming place. A shady garden is more inviting when pools of dappled light illuminate its farthest reaches—they draw you toward them and give added depth. In

above Light filtering through
a corkscrew willow creates a
delicate tracery pattern on the
water in a shallow galvanized
trough. The stones highlight a
subtle composition that might
otherwise go unnoticed.

right The stone table on this
terrace provides a cool, shady
place to eat outdoor meals during
the day. When evening comes, the
lanterns hanging above the table
are lit to make the perfect spot to
enjoy an alfresco dinner.

the absence of direct light, a similar effect can be achieved with
variegated foliage or white flowers. Conversely, sunny gardens need
areas of shade for definition.

Light and shade are not only about how the garden looks, they
are also about how it feels—in other words, warmth and coolness.
In a predominantly shady garden, it is nice to have at least a patch
of sun to bask in, and in a sunny garden the shade of an occasional
tree is a welcome retreat from soaring summer temperatures.
These days, most of us are more careful about exposure to the
direct sun, especially around noon, but it is always pleasant to have
somewhere to sit that catches the early morning or evening sun,
even if it isn't close to the house. A distant bench positioned to
catch the last rays of the setting sun will lure you outside to enjoy

A distant bench positioned to catch the last rays of the setting sun will lure you outside to enjoy the peace and quiet of the garden. What better way to switch off after a hard day's work?

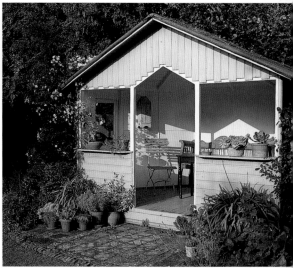

left **The play of light on the water of this natural stone swimming pool is far more enticing than it would be on a more conventional tiled pool. Areas of sun and shade around the pool provide relaxing spots for both sun-worshippers and shade-lovers alike.**

above left **A rustic lantern provides subtle lighting for a romantic outdoor dinner.**

above right **Perfectly positioned to catch the setting sun, this gazebo is the ideal place to retreat to at the end of the day to enjoy some peace and quiet.**

the peace and quiet of the garden. What better way to unwind after a hard day's work?

When buying a new home, it is always worth asking the sellers where the sun rises and sets. Better still, try to visit the property at different times of day so you can observe the light for yourself. When I bought my house, it wasn't until I moved in that I realized that, because it is situated on the wooded western slope of a valley, it loses the sun quite early in the evening. This means that it is wonderfully sheltered from the prevailing winds, but I do miss wandering around the garden in the warm evening sunshine.

The nighttime garden is a place of darkness and mystery, so maybe it isn't surprising that many people are reluctant to

Lanterns, candles, torches, and mini tree lights can be used to light alfresco meals or give the garden atmosphere on special occasions.

venture out into their gardens after dark, even though they are so familiar during the day. Unfortunately, the only artificial lighting that exists in most gardens is for security purposes, and it is about as flattering to its surroundings as the lighting in an underground parking lot. Although installing well-designed garden lighting is quite an expensive process, its transforming effect is worth every penny. It can make an ordinary garden look quite magical, with washes and pools of light making the familiar seem quite new, and will greatly extend the time you spend outdoors. Expert advice is recommended; this is a specialized subject. Solar lighting that needs no wiring is becoming more common, but in general the lamps give off very little light

and are not very attractively designed. If and when the technology and the design improve, they may open up many new possibilities for garden lighting.

On a much more modest scale, lanterns, candles, torches, and mini tree lights can be used to light alfresco meals or give the garden atmosphere on special occasions. Mini lights can be twined through plants, around arbors, and up plant supports if there is an outdoor power source, but make sure the lights are rated for outdoor use. Floating candles transform a pond, and a candlelit table on the terrace is the perfect setting for a romantic meal. Chinese paper lanterns, hung from trees and illuminated by votives, are both exotic and practical.

opposite left In this Los Angeles garden, mini tree lights strung through the climbing plants on the arbor echo the city lights that twinkle far below. Crystal decorations have been hung from the arbor to catch the light. Comfortable chairs complete this perfect spot for outdoor entertaining.

opposite right A tiny London courtyard comes to life at night when it is lit by votive candles in Moroccan tea glasses, lanterns, and a shiny copper bowl.

above The highly burnished copper bowl glows with reflected light, amplifying the effect of the votives.

right This group of glass candle holders is both pretty and practical—the candles are safely contained and will burn better protected from any drafts.

scent and sound

fragrant plants

herbs

cool water and rustling breezes

Close your eyes in a peaceful garden and its magic
continues as your other senses are soothed and fine-
tuned. The scent of perfumed flowers and aromatic
herbs hangs in the air, and free of visual distraction,
will envelop you. As you breathe in the fragrance, you
will become more aware of the soothing sounds around
you—splashing water, rustling foliage, or birdsong.

right A cottage garden overflowing with flowers would be greatly diminished without fragrance. As beautiful as the roses are to look at, it isn't until we bury our noses in the blooms that we really respond to their beauty— even with our eyes closed.

fragrant plants

In our relationship with plants, fragrance is often as significant as appearance. There are plants of modest appearance that we grow purely for their scent—plants like mignonette, *Reseda odorata*, and night-scented stocks, *Matthiola longipetala*—while there are others that disappoint if they fail to smell as we expect. Roses or sweet peas with no scent are diminished by their lack of fragrance.

Our love affair with scented flowers has a long history. The Egyptians grew the sacred lotus for its voluptuous and narcotic scent. The Romans were so enamored of the rose that they filled fountains with its petals, and the Persians invented the process of distillation to extract the essential oil from roses. During the Middle Ages in Europe, scented flowers were given as love tokens, and some also had religious significance. The lily in particular was a symbol of fertility and purity, and for centuries any painting of the Annunciation would include a lily held by the Madonna or an angel.

Our sense of smell works differently from the other senses because the olfactory nerves head straight for the emotions. Scent and memory are inextricably entangled, and a familiar fragrance will always recall past events. If you first smelled lavender in your grandmother's garden on a sunny day during a happy childhood summer, then lavender will recreate that feeling of happiness, while a

PLANTS WITH FRAGRANT FLOWERS

Winter: *Hamamelis* (witch hazel)

Sarcococca humilis (sweet box)

Viburnum x *bodnantense* 'Dawn'

Spring: *Convallaria majalis* (lily of the valley)

Daphne odora 'Aureomarginata'

Mahonia aquifolium (Oregon grape)

Summer: *Hesperis matronalis* (sweet rocket)

Jasmine, common or star

Lathyrus odoratus (sweet pea)

Lavandula (lavender)

Lilium candidum (Madonna lily)

Lonicera (honeysuckle)

Matthiola longipetala (night-scented stock)

Paeonia lactiflora (peony)

Philadelphus coronarius (mock orange)

Phlox paniculata (border phlox)

Reseda odorata (mignonette)

Rosa gallica var. *officinalis* and others

heart broken under a honeysuckle will always associate its sweet fragrance with sadness. Before planting a scented garden, it is interesting to check your own responses to the plants you have in mind. Scent is so subjective that other people's recommendations are not always appropriate.

The volatile oils that give flowers their fragrance are at their most concentrated in the plant early in the day. This is why roses that are gathered for perfumes are harvested at dawn. As the sun warms the flowers, the oils evaporate and the fragrance is diffused into the surrounding air. When you walk through a sunny garden enjoying its sweet scents, you are literally breathing in perfumed air.

left **In a wildflower meadow, a beautiful white rose scrambles through a neighboring tree—evidence of a long-abandoned garden.**

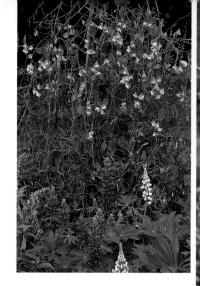

Garden scents change with the seasons. Even in midwinter, fragrant plants perfume the air. Witch hazel will stop you in your tracks, as will the scent of winter-flowering *Viburnum* and *Sarcococca*. Plant them close to a well-used path or terrace, unless you are in the habit of wandering around the garden in midwinter. In early spring, the Oregon grape *Mahonia* and *Daphne odora* 'Aureomarginata' are deliciously scented, while lily of the valley is best picked and brought indoors to appreciate its lovely perfume. There are, of course, plenty of scented bulbs, too—daffodils, jonquils, narcissus, hyacinths, and there are even tulips that have a sweet freesia scent, 'Ballerina' being one of the finest.

Once summer arrives, there are so many fragrances to choose from—the bubble-gum scent of the mock orange, the citrus scent of peony flowers, the musky fragrance of phlox. As at the perfume counter of a department store, you can take your pick of everything from the subtle to the overpowering.

Scented flowers are best appreciated in a sunny, sheltered garden—the sun concentrates the oils, and shelter means that the scent hangs in the air rather than being blown away by the wind. The effect can be accentuated further by growing plants over bowers, arbors, and arches—all of which will trap the scent within them. A mixture of roses, honeysuckle, and jasmines—both *Jasminum officinale*, common jasmine, and the star jasmine, *Trachelospermum jasminoides*, will provide long-lasting fragrance. Although their season is quite short, scented wisterias have a dramatic beauty, especially when the blooms hang down

above **The pink and white blooms of this old-fashioned sweet pea are quite small but intensely fragrant. Fortunately, many of the larger-flowered modern sweet peas are now having fragrance bred back into them, but it is always worth adding a few old varieties as well. To appreciate the scent of sweet peas, you really need to grow them yourself—once they are picked, the fragrance fades.**

right **Not all roses have a fine scent. The 'Peace' rose may have a perfect, delicate beauty, but sadly its fragrance does not match its looks.**

far right **Like a parfumier, the gardener can combine scented plants so that their different aromas blend into a delicious fragrance. In this garden, honeysuckle, roses, and lilies combine together in a heady perfume.**

within an arbor. On a pathway fringed with fragrant plants, allow them to fall across its margins so that you brush against them and release their fragrance.

Of all scented flowers, roses are probably the most universally popular, but there is an enormous variability in their scent as well as their other qualities. The four roses considered best for the making of rose oil, and therefore the most fragrant, are 'Belle de Crécy,' 'Louise Odier,' 'Madame Isaac Pereire,' and 'Roseraie de l'Haÿ,' but it is worth remembering that these old varieties are not always repeat flowering, and they can have rather messy habits. Many modern roses are now bred to have the virtues of good scent, good growth habit, and disease resistance.

Lavender is the quintessential cottage garden flower, but it needs the right conditions to grow well. It is a Mediterranean plant, so give it the full sun and good drainage it loves and it will thrive. It isn't the cold that kills lavender during the winter—it's the combination of cold and wet that is lethal. 'Hidcote' is the most popular lavender variety—its deep color and compact habit make it an ideal choice for lining paths and growing in containers.

Scented flowers are best appreciated in a sunny, sheltered garden—the sun concentrates the oils, and shelter means that the scent hangs in the air rather than being blown away by the wind. Grow plants over bowers, arbors, and arches to trap the scent.

opposite The flower of the French lavender *Lavandula stoechas* is very different in appearance from common lavender, but has a similar fragrance. 'Helmsdale' is a new cultivar with a striking dark burgundy flower.

above A rose-covered arch and a lavender-lined pathway lead to a rustic bench—the perfect place to sit and drink in the scents that surround you.

right A grass path leads down the center of a fragrant lavender walk. To keep it looking this good, it is essential to trim the lavender as soon as the flowers start to fade—otherwise, gaps will open up in the bushes, and they will start to look leggy. Lavender is relatively short-lived, so it is a good idea to take cuttings from the second year on. You can never have too many lavender plants.

herbs

Herbs are perfect companions in the peaceful garden. Their reassuring presence and aromatic qualities hark back to times when we had a much more direct connection with the plants we grew—they were our food and our medicine. For many of us, herbs are now the only useful plants that we still cultivate and use as an everyday ingredient.

We respond very positively to the word "herb," as we do to many of the properties of the herbs themselves —for centuries they have been used to heal, soothe, cleanse, and calm, as well as being much-loved flavorings in our food. Our relationship with them is often reflected in their folk names—names like bee balm (*Melissa officinalis*), knitbone (*Symphytum officinale*), eyebright (*Euphrasia officinalis*), and feverfew (*Chrysanthemum parthenium*).

Although the modern herb garden is harvested mainly for culinary herbs or sometimes for ingredients used in the making of potpourri and lavender sachets, many of us also grow other herbs. Herbs remain more than pleasantly fragrant plants that decorate our gardens and enliven our foods. This does not mean though that they are all equally benign, and anyone cultivating herbs beyond the most well-known

left Creeping thyme and other low-growing herbs are perfect for the spaces between paving or on a terrace.

above right Many of the traditional folk cures have been proved to have real value. Sage, so named for its reputation as a herb for improving memory, is now being used in the treatment of Alzheimer's disease.

right Although it is a nice idea to put a chair in the middle of a carpet of fragrant herbs, do it with caution. Bees love these herbs as much as we do, so you risk being stung.

above left **Rosemary**
tumbles over terracotta
pots, conjuring up the
colors and scent of
Tuscany.

above right **The distinctive**
flavor of caraway seeds
is one of those tastes that
you either love or hate.
For some it evokes
nostalgic memories
of grandma's cakes.

opposite **A simple plank**
bench is a perfect excuse
to linger among the herbs.
The fragrance is always
at its most intense after
noon, when the volatile
oils have evaporated
from the herbs into
the surrounding air.

varieties should be familiar with their properties
before doing anything other than admiring how
they grow in the garden.

If you are planning to lay out an herb plot,
take into account the conditions that the
different herbs require to grow well. The
Mediterranean herbs—which include sage,
rosemary, thyme, oregano, and marjoram—need
really good drainage and a hot sunny site. Think
of their natural habitat—the arid, stony coastlines
and hills of France, Italy, and Greece—and you
will realize that a deeply cultivated soil is far too
rich a diet for them. They also hate to have their
roots sitting in water, so lots of added sand is
essential in all but the stoniest soils. However,
there are other herbs that welcome moist soil
and a degree of shade. Mint, parsley, and lemon
balm will all do better in fertile soil in a lightly
shaded site. Mint and lemon balm need to be
contained in some way or they will rapidly

Enjoy herbs' aromatic qualities in the garden. Plant creeping thyme and rosemary in between paving slabs, and you will release their fragrance as you walk along the path.

above left **Basil** is a quintessential summer herb, redolent of sunny days. Here purple basil grows in an old can.

above right **Thyme flowers** attract bees and other beneficial insects. Sit near a plant and you will hear it hum.

opposite above left **Culinary thyme** should always be included in a cook's herb

garden. As soon as it has finished flowering, give the plant a trim to encourage new shoots and stop it from getting too leggy.

opposite below left **Creeping thyme** loves to grow in a hot, dry place where it can tumble over a wall or the edge of a container.

opposite right **Sage** is an essential culinary herb, good in meat dishes.

overwhelm their less rampant neighbors. Traditionally, they were planted in buckets with a hole in the base. A modern equivalent is to cut the bottom out of a large plastic pot, sink it in the ground with just the rim showing above soil level, and plant into this. Mint and lemon balm spread via runners along the top of the soil, so this method will keep them contained.

Even in the tiniest herb garden, try to find space for the classic culinary herbs—parsley, sage, rosemary, and thyme—and a standard bay tree as well. In mild areas they can all be planted in the ground; elsewhere, the less hardy plants, especially rosemary and bay, may need to be planted in pots and moved indoors. Always use a potting soil with some added sand. This is much more suitable than soil containing peat or peat substitutes, which has a tendency to dry out in summer and become waterlogged in winter.

above Sage comes in many varieties, some purely decorative and some palatable. *Salvia officinalis* is the culinary sage. This variegated form, *Salvia officinalis* 'Icterina,' tastes as good as it looks. A tea made from the leaves with honey added is good for sore throats. The petals of the flowers, removed from the leafy calyx, taste delicious.

right The non-flowering form of chamomile, 'Treneague,' is ideal for lawns or along paths. Taller-growing chamomiles are cultivated for their flowers, which are used to make soothing teas and other herbal remedies.

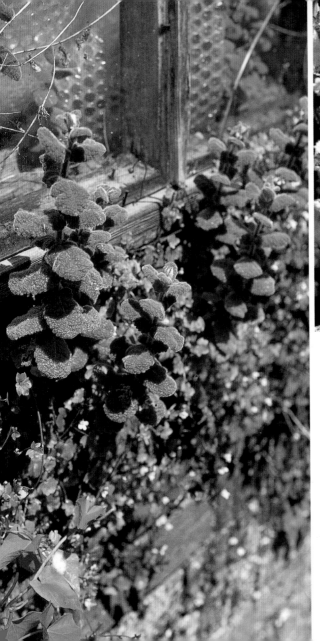

this page Mint is a refreshing and stimulating herb. Like sage, it comes in many varieties with different uses. While the wooly mint (left) can be used in the kitchen, many varieties, such as variegated mint (above), tend to be too perfumed to make enjoyable eating. Mint needs regular feeding and plenty of water to keep it growing well.

right **A perennial sweet pea twines its way through a rosemary bush. Rosemary is a highly aromatic herb, which bears its fragile blue flowers in the depths of winter. Frequent picking of the stems keeps the plant attractively bushy—left to its own devices, it has a tendency to become leggy.**

far right **The feathery foliage of fennel contrasts pleasingly with the shape of the flowering thyme in the foreground. Its delicate stems rise above its surroundings, lending height to the herb bed.**

FRAGRANT HERBS

Aloysia triphylla (lemon verbena)

Anethum graveolens (dill)

Artemisia dracunculus (tarragon)

Borago officinalis (borage)

Carum carvi (caraway)

Chamaemelum nobile (chamomile)

Coriandrum sativum (coriander)

Foeniculum vulgare (fennel)

Laurus nobilis (bay)

Melissa officinalis (lemon balm)

Mentha (mint) | *Ocimum basilicum* (basil)

Origanum vulgare (marjoram)

Petroselinum (parsley)

Rosmarinus officinalis (rosemary)

Salvia officinalis (sage)

Satureja hortensis (summer savory)

Satureja montana (winter savory)

Thymus vulgaris (common thyme)

Once you have grown lemon verbena, you will never want to be without it. Brush past it and the air is filled with a delicate citrus fragrance. Its leaves can be used to make a refreshing tea and as a flavoring in fruit salads and cakes. It will survive outdoors in mild areas. A sun-baked corner at the base of a wall or a hot bank with poor, dry soil is what it likes best. This is another Mediterranean herb that hates to be wet in winter. Don't prune it until the first green shoots are showing in the spring. Grown in a pot, it can be left to dry right out in the greenhouse— start watering moderately when spring is well advanced.

Many herbs are equally happy among flowers, so even if you haven't got an area dedicated to herbs, you can still enjoy their aromatic qualities in the peaceful garden. Plant creeping thyme and rosemary in between paving slabs and you will release their fragrance as you walk along.

cool water and rustling breezes

When we include a pond, a rill, or a fountain in a peaceful garden, it can make us more aware of the essential role of water in our lives. As we listen to its gentle splashing or gaze into a reflecting pool, the water's presence is both reassuring and calming. Breezes ripple the water's surface and rustle through the surrounding foliage.

For those of us who live in temperate climates where rain falls regularly and unlimited water flows from our faucets, it is easy to forget that water is a precious and often scarce commodity in many parts of the world. Historically, gardens could only exist where there was a reliable water source or where people had learned to control and conserve water. When the great gardens of the past were laid out, the control of water was frequently a central theme. The Persians piped water from distant mountains to make the desert bloom in gardens where splashing fountains and gently flowing rills cooled the dry air. In Europe the aristocracy and wealthy landowners employed the likes of Capability Brown and Humphrey Repton to manipulate the landscape,

left The seat built into the bank next to this pond is an invitation to sit down and enjoy the view. The fountain could be improved—oddly positioned and standing above the water, it detracts from rather than adds to the scene. There are better ways to produce the sound of splashing water.

right Carefully placed rocks and naturalistic planting, including *Iris pseudacorus* 'Variegata' in the foreground, create the illusion of a stream tumbling down a hillside.

A great benefit of water in the garden is the wildlife it attracts —dragonflies that hover above the water on iridescent wings, birds that drink and bathe in it, small mammals that visit, amphibians that take up residence, and tiny water striders that scoot over the surface.

above This dark, rectangular pond needs no embellishment. Its magnificent setting and its reflective qualities have a restrained perfection.

right It isn't always necessary to re-landscape the garden in order to introduce water. A pond in a pot in a tiny garden conjures up the feeling of an inviting jungle pool, surrounded by rocky outcrops and lush vegetation.

right **In a contemporary garden that is severely architectural, an alcove in the wall contains the simplest of water features. Water splashes down into a rectangular trough from a spout set in the wall and then overflows into a lower pool. In a garden devoid of natural shade, this cool corner must be a welcome relief.**

damming rivers and employing hundreds of workers over decades to dig ornamental lakes or create canals. In the gardens of Versailles, Villa d'Este, and Chatsworth, water engineering reached its zenith with the creation of magnificent cascades and fountains. In these gardens, water was more important than plants.

Today water is generally used on a more modest scale, even in public spaces. We all have the technology, most of us have adequate water, and with nothing to prove, it seems that many of us are content to restrict the water in our gardens to little more than an outside faucet and a hose or a concealed irrigation system. Expense is, understandably, an important consideration. Unless you are fortunate enough to have natural water running through your garden, the addition of all but the most modest of ponds is going to involve major landscaping work. It is wise to consult an expert in these matters—a poorly designed water feature is worse than none at all, especially in a peaceful garden where all the elements should induce calm rather than irritation. Ponds that are too shallow cause the most problems. They have a tendency to turn green at the drop of a hat and rapidly fill with great curtains of algae encouraged by the warm, shallow water. Overhanging trees that drop their leaves will clog and pollute a pond—admittedly, water can look very pretty in a shady spot, but such a pond will need netting in the fall and regular cleaning, or it will degenerate into a smelly, stagnant bog.

As with other design aspects of the peaceful garden, the way water is used should be appropriate to the setting. A formal symmetrical garden requires a formal pond. Traditional materials that echo existing features are a safe bet, but provided the shape and the dimensions are right, the use of contemporary materials can offer a more interesting solution. Simple, clean lines work best in a modern urban garden where the inclusion of falling or running water effectively masks the sound of traffic and freshens the air. In a country garden, a natural pond will blend into the landscape and look as if it has always been there. This type of pond takes time to establish and balance, but it is worth the effort and is ultimately a more attractive solution than digging a hole and installing a preformed pond bought at a garden center. For some reason, they are generally bright blue and strangely amebic in shape, and it is hard to imagine any location where one would look appropriate.

Before embarking on any water feature, it is essential to consider safety. If small children regularly use or visit the garden, open water of any description is potentially dangerous. There will be little enjoyment if you have to be constantly on guard to avert tragedy. This does not mean that water must be entirely excluded —a pebble fountain is a simple and safe way of introducing water into a small garden, or better still a water spout coming out of a wall and falling through a grate or onto stones at ground level, is both safe and entertaining for children.

One of the great benefits of having water in the garden is the wildlife that it attracts—the dragonflies that hover above the water with their iridescent wings, the birds that drink and bathe in it, small mammals that visit, amphibians that take

above A sheet of reeded stainless steel provides a textured surface down which the water can flow, creating bubbles and movement in the water to keep the fish healthy.

left A basement area outside a townhouse has been turned from a dingy, unattractive, and unused space into a Japanese-inspired water garden. Underwater lighting has been set into the trough, so its calming presence is not overlooked in the evening. Materials are thoroughly urban and the planting is simple— bamboo, cotoneaster, and an arum lily.

up residence, and the tiny water striders that scoot across the surface. If you need an excuse to linger in your peaceful garden, these creatures will provide it. Natural ponds provide the best environment with their shallow, gently sloping sides where marginal plants soften the edges and provide suitable wildlife habitats. A comfortable seat nearby will encourage you to sit and watch the life of the pond, and if the pond is large enough, a rowboat will allow a closer look.

Swimming pools can be a blight on the landscape, but a new development with its roots in Europe is set to change their appearance and their environmental impact in a dramatic way. Swimming ponds originated in Austria, where designers were looking for a way to make swimming pools wildlife friendly and less obtrusive. A central swimming pool is enclosed in an open tank, the top of which is just below water level, and this is above left **Water dribbles gently over these stones through a pipe inserted in a hole drilled through the stack. Even when the water isn't flowing, they have a sculptural quality.**

below left **A large ceramic bowl has been made into an eye-catching illuminated water feature.**

right **Glass bricks were used to make this unusual water trough on a London roof terrace. Filled with pebbles, and with water splashing from above, there is not a plant in sight, but nonetheless there is a pleasant contrast of shapes and textures in the arrangement.**

surrounded by a gently sloping pond twice the size of the swimming area. Both pool and pond are lined with a dark, heavy-duty butyl liner. The pond is then lined with a deep layer of gravel and planted with a wide variety of aquatic and marginal plants, which act as oxygenators and water purifiers, doing away with the need for a filtration system. Once the swimming pond has settled down and plants are growing well, there is little maintenance involved, and wildlife and humans coexist happily in their different areas of the pond. A pier leads from the bank to the central swimming pool, where you can enjoy all the best aspects of swimming in natural water without scraping your knees on concealed rocks or getting tangled in weeds.

Selective planting around the margins of any pool or pond adds immeasurably to the atmosphere. Waterlilies love deep, still water and are suitable for both formal and natural ponds. Marginal plants grow best in the

The way water is used should be appropriate to the setting. Simple, clean lines work best in a modern urban garden where the inclusion of falling or running water effectively masks the sound of traffic and freshens the air. In a country garden, a natural pond will look as if it has always been there.

shallows, where their roots are in wet or boggy ground and their leaves and flowers are in the sun. In addition to flowering plants such as arum lilies, candelabra primulas, astilbes, and Siberian irises, there are foliage plants to sway in the breezes moving across the pond.

It is possible to create the illusion of flowing water in a garden with a still pond or even one with no water at all, using the sound of the wind rustling through leaves. In France, the wind blowing through the tall stands of poplar trees that punctuate the landscape sounds exactly like a rapidly flowing river. The giant grass *Arundo donax* and bamboos catch the breeze and emulate the sound of a babbling brook.

The sounds of plants are all around us, once we have tuned in to them. I can stand in my own very sheltered garden with barely a breeze ruffling my hair while the sound of the wind roars through the trees on the rim of the valley, wondering at the power of nature. Closer in, on a much smaller scale, I can hear the gentle popping of seedheads on a *Geranium palmatum* as it disperses its seeds, the rustle of dry leaves underfoot, and in the kitchen garden, the gentle clatter of ripening bean pods as they rattle against one another. These small, intimate sounds help focus the mind and sharpen the senses.

Some sounds are so slight that they are barely audible, but when they are combined with movement, even they become apparent. This is particularly true with ornamental grasses—their gentle rustling could go entirely unnoticed, but the swaying of the leaves draws the eye and encourages closer examination. These small discoveries and pleasures contain within them the essential elements that can make any garden a peaceful place and a personal sanctuary.

far left Bamboo looks wonderful close to ponds or streams, where the rustling of the wind in their foliage adds atmosphere. Select the variety carefully, as many are rampant, and their sharp shoots can pierce the strongest of pond liners.

left Ornamental grasses, like this *Stipa tenuissima* planted among pink astrantias, pick up every breeze and bring movement to the garden.

right From left to right, the bamboos *Phyllostachys aurea* 'Holochrysa', *P. aurea*, and *P. aurea* 'Koi' have contrasting stems and leaves. In a garden without water, the sound of the breeze rippling through their leaves creates the illusion of its presence.

Architects, designers, and nurseries whose work and gardens are featured in this book:

Key: a=above, b=below, c=center, l=left, r=right

Bedmar & Shi Designers Pte Ltd
12a Keong Saik Road
Singapore 089119
t. +65 22 77117
f. +65 22 77695
*A Singapore-based firm
established in 1980,
specializing in residential
projects and also in interior
design, mainly for
restaurants and offices.*
Pages 15, 38–39, 87, 131.

Jonathan Bell
11 Sinclair Gardens
London W14 0AU
UK
t. +44 020 7371 3455
e. jb@jbell.demon.co.uk
Pages 18–19, 48, 86.

Susan Berger & Helen Phillips
Town Garden Design
69 Kingsdown Parade
Bristol BS6 5UG
UK
t./f. +44 0117 942 3843
Pages 26–27, 47.

Tania Compton
e. taniacompton@
madasafish.com
Pages 40–41, 52–53.

Cooper/Taggart Designs
t. 323 254 3048
e. coopertaggart@
earthlink.net
Pages 88r, 106l.

De Brinkhof Garden and Nursery
Dorpsstrat 46
6616 AJ Hernen
Holland
t. +31 487 531 486
*Nursery and garden open
Friday and Saturday from
10am to 5pm, from April
until the end of September.
A small nursery specializing
in old-fashioned and
unusual varieties of hardy
perennial.*
Pages 13, 21, 34–35, 44b,
46a, 105r.

Pierre & Sandrine Degrugillier
Le Mas de Flore
Lagnes 84800
France
t. +33 04 90 20 37 96
*Antique and made-to-order
furniture.*
Page 98.

Great Dixter Nurseries
Northiam
Rye
East Sussex TN31 6PH
UK
t. +44 01797 253107
f. +44 01797 252879
e. greatdixter@
compuserve.com
Page 42.

Isabelle C. Greene, F.A.S.L.A.
Isabelle Greene & Associates
2613 De la Vina Street
Santa Barbara
CA 93105
t. 805 569 4045
e. icgreene@aol.com
*Landscape architects and
land planners.*
Page 14.

Gruga Park Botanic Gardens
Kulshammerweg 32 D 451
49 Essen
Germany
Page 34.

HDRA's Yalding Organic Gardens
Yalding Organic Gardens
Benover Road
Yalding, near Maidstone
Kent ME18 6EX
UK
t. +44 01622 814650
www.hdra.org.uk
*HDRA (Henry Doubleday
Research Association), the
Organic Association-
registered charity
researching and promoting
organic gardening, farming,
and food. Open 10am to
5pm Wednesday to Sunday,
May to September, and
weekends during April and
October. Also open Easter
and Bank Holiday Mondays.*
Page 117l.

Judy M. Horton Garden Design
136 1/2 North Larchmont
Boulevard, Suite B
Los Angeles
CA 9004
t. 323 462 1412
f. 323 462 8979
e. info@jmhgarden
design.com
Pages 2, 28, 88l.

Jan Howard
Room in the Garden
Oak Cottage
Furzen Lane
Ellens Green, Rudgwick
West Sussex RH12 3AR
UK
t. +44 01403 823958
*Manufacturers of elegant
designs in rusted iron.
Garden design services
by Jan Howard.
Catalog available.*
Page 62l.

Ivan Hicks
t./f. +44 01963 210886
e. ivan@theedge88.
fsnet.co.uk
*Garden and landscape
designer, land artist.*
Pages 58l, 62r.

Iden Croft Herbs
Staplehurst, Kent, UK
www.herbs-uk.com
Pages 59, 67, 69a, 77,
110–111, 114–115, 116,
120–121.

Japanese Garden & Bonsai
Nursery
St Mawgan
Cornwall
UK
t. +44 01637 860116
Pages 45, 129.

Johnson-Naylor Interior
Architecture
t. +44 020 7490 8885
Pages 4r, 17, 24–25,
48–49, 83r, 89l, 102.

Judy Kameon
Elysian Landscapes
724 Academy Road
Los Angeles
CA 90012
t. 323 226 9588
f. 323 226 1191
www.plainair.com
*Garden design and
outdoor furniture.*
Page 134b.

La Bambouserie de
Prafrance
301040 par Anduze
France
t. +33 68 61 70 47
Pages 108, 137.

Peter & Pam Lewis
Sticky Wicket
Buckland Newton
Dorchester
Dorset DT2 7BY
UK
t./f. +44 01300 345476
*Garden design, restoration,
and management.*
Pages 8–9, 22l, 23, 36–37,
64–65, 112–113, 136–137.

Dale Loth Architects
1 Cliff Road
London NW1 9AJ
UK
t. +44 020 7485 4003
f. +44 020 7284 4490
www.dalelotharchitects.co.uk
Pages 132–133.

Christina Oates
Secret Garden Designs
Fovant Hut
Fovant, nr. Salisbury
Wiltshire SP3 5LN
UK
t. +44 01722 714756
www.secretgarden
  designs.co.uk
*Garden designer Christina
Oates specializes in
imaginative and yet down-
to-earth consultancy visits
and concept plans.*
Pages 10, 44ar, 69b, 73.

Sarah Raven's Cutting
Garden
Perch Hill Farm
Brightling, Robertsbridge
East Sussex TN32 5HP
UK
t. +44 01424 838181
f. +44 01424 838571
e. info@thecutting
  garden.com
www.thecuttinggarden.com
Page 66.

Michael Reeves Interiors
33 Mossop Street
London SW3 2NB
UK
t. +44 020 7225 2501
f. +44 020 7225 3060
Pages 84–85.

Suzanne Rheinstein
Associates
817 North Hilldale Avenue
West Hollywood
CA 90069
t. 323 931 340
and Hollyhock Hilldale
Address as above
*Garden antiques and
accessories.*
e. Hollyhockinc@aol.com
Pages 2, 28, 81l.

Rowden Gardens
Brentor
nr. Tavistock
Devon PL19 0NG
UK
t./f. +44 01822 810275
Page 81.

Marc Schoellen
35 route de Colmar-Berg
L-7525 Mersch
Grand-Duché de
Luxembourg
t. +352 327 269
*Garden historian and
amateur garden designer.*
Pages 25, 68, 70, 80–81b.

Roberto Silva
128 Hemingford Road
London N1 1DE
UK
t. +44 020 7700 7487
e. landrob7@aol.com
Pages 3, 20–21, 58r, 82, 90l.

Enrica Stabile
l'Utile e il Dilettevole
via Carlo Maria Maggi 6
20154 Milano
Italy
t. +39 234 53 60 86
www.enricastabile.com

*Antique furniture, garden
furniture, decorative objects,
soft furnishings, textiles.*
Pages 7, 57a, 98, 100, 103,
104.

Sally Storey
John Cullen Lighting
585 Kings Road
London SW6 2EH
UK
t. +44 020 7371 5400
*A wide range of practical
contemporary light fittings
as well as innovative made-
to-measure lighting design.*
Pages 16–17, 134a.

Derry Watkins
Special Plants
Greenways Lane
Cold Ashton
Chippenham
Wiltshire SN14 8LA
UK
t. +44 01225 891686
e. specialplants@bigfoot.com
www.specialplants.net
*Opening hours 10.30am
to 4.30pm March to
September, other times
by arrangement.*
Page 128.

Whitelaw Turkington
Landscape Architects
t. +44 020 7820 0388
Pages 4r, 17, 24–25,
48–49, 83r, 89l, 102.

Stephen Woodhams
378 Brixton Road
London SW9 7AW
UK
t. +44 020 7346 5656
Page 135.

Picture credits

All photography by Melanie Eclare unless stated otherwise.
Key: a=above, b=below, r=right, l=left, c=center, ph=photographer

Page 2 garden of interior designer Suzanne Rheinstein, designed by Judy M. Horton; **3** a garden in south London designed by Roberto Silva; **4l** Niall Manning & Alastair Morton's garden, Dunard, Fintry, Scotland G63 0EX; **4c** ph Pia Tryde; **4r** Fiona Naylor and Peter Marlow's roof garden in London designed by Fiona Naylor and landscape architect Lindsey Whitelaw; **5** ph Pia Tryde; **7** ph Christopher Drake/Enrica Stabile's house, Le Thor, Provence; garden bench & cushions, l'Utile e il Dilettevole; **8–9** Sticky Wicket wildlife garden near Dorchester, designed and created by Peter and Pam Lewis; **10** Fovant Hut Garden near Salisbury in Wiltshire was created by garden designer Christina Oates together with her husband Nigel and is open to the public; **12** Connie Haydon's garden in Dorset; **13** the garden and nursery De Brinkhof of Riet Brinkhof and Joop Van Den Berk; **14** Carol Valentine's garden in California, designed by Isabelle Greene, F.A.S.L.A., a California landscape architect and planner; **15** ph Andrew Wood/'Melwani House' designed by Bedmar & Shi designers in Singapore; **16–17** a house in Chelsea, lighting designed by Sally Storey; **17** Fiona Naylor and Peter Marlow's roof garden in London designed by Fiona Naylor and landscape architect Lindsey Whitelaw; **18–19** a garden in London designed by Jonathan Bell; **20–21** a garden in south London designed by Roberto Silva; **21** the garden and nursery De Brinkhof of Riet Brinkhof and Joop Van Den Berk; **22l** Sticky Wicket wildlife garden near Dorchester, designed and created by Peter and Pam Lewis; **22r** Niall Manning and Alastair Morton's garden, Dunard, Fintry, Scotland G63 0EX; **23** Sticky Wicket wildlife garden near Dorchester, designed and created by Peter and Pam Lewis; **24–25** Fiona Naylor and Peter Marlow's roof garden in London designed by Fiona Naylor and landscape architect Lindsey Whitelaw; **25** Marc Schoellen's garden in Luxembourg called 'La Bergerie'; **26–27** the garden of James Morris in Bristol designed by Sue Berger & Helen Phillips; **28** garden of interior designer Suzanne Rheinstein, designed by Judy M. Horton; **29** Jim Reynolds's garden 'Butterstream', Co. Meath, Ireland; **30** Connie Haydon's garden in Dorset; **31** Jim Reynolds's garden 'Butterstream', Co. Meath, Ireland; **32l** Niall Manning & Alastair Morton's garden, Dunard, Fintry, Scotland G63 0EX; **32r** Jim Reynolds's garden 'Butterstream', Co. Meath, Ireland; **33** Niall Manning & Alastair Morton's garden, Dunard, Fintry, Scotland G63 0EX; **34** ph Andrea Jones/Gruga Park Botanic Gardens; **34–35** the garden and nursery De Brinkhof of Riet Brinkhof and Joop Van Den Berk; **36–37** Sticky Wicket wildlife garden near Dorchester, designed and created by Peter and Pam Lewis; **38–39** ph Andrew Wood/'Melwani House' designed by Bedmar & Shi designers in Singapore; **40–41** Peter and Sandra Aitken-Quack's garden at Ham Cross Farm near Tisbury, designed by Tania Compton; **42** ph Andrea Jones/Great Dixter Nurseries; **43** ph Caroline Hughes/John and Joan Ward's garden in London; **44al** Jim Reynolds's garden 'Butterstream', Co. Meath, Ireland; **44ar** Fovant Hut Garden near Salisbury in Wiltshire was created by garden designer Christina Oates together with her husband Nigel and is open to the public; **44b** the garden and nursery De Brinkhof of Riet Brinkhof and Joop Van Den Berk; **45** ph Andrea Jones/Japanese Garden & Bonsai Nursery; **46a** the garden and nursery De Brinkhof of Riet Brinkhof and Joop Van Den Berk; **46b** Mr. and Mrs. James Hepworth's garden in Herefordshire; **47** the garden of James Morris in Bristol designed by Sue Berger & Helen Phillips; **48** a garden in London designed by Jonathan Bell; **48–49** Fiona Naylor and Peter Marlow's roof garden in London designed by Fiona Naylor and landscape architect Lindsey Whitelaw; **50** Mr. and Mrs. James Hepworth's garden in Herefordshire; **51** ph Polly Wreford/Mary Foley's house in Connecticut; **52–53** Peter and Sandra Aitken-Quack's garden at Ham Cross Farm near Tisbury, designed by Tania Compton; **54** Jim Reynolds's garden 'Butterstream', Co. Meath, Ireland; **54–55** ph Chris Tubbs/Maureen Kelly's house in the Catskills, New York; **56** the Farrell family, Woodnewton; **57b** ph Pia Tryde; **57a** ph Christopher Drake/Enrica Stabile's house, Le Thor, Provence; garden bench & cushions, l'Utile e il Dilettevole; **58l** Mart Barlow's garden designed by Ivan Hicks; **58r** a garden in south London designed by Roberto Silva; **59** ph Caroline

Hughes/Iden Croft Herbs; **60** Hutton Wilkinson's garden designed by Tony Duquette; **61l** Mirabel Osler's garden in Ludlow, Shropshire; **61r** Hutton Wilkinson's garden designed by Tony Duquette; **62l** Jan Howard's garden in Sussex; **62r** Mart Barlow's garden designed by Ivan Hicks; **63** Mirabel Osler's garden in Ludlow, Shropshire; **64–65** Sticky Wicket wildlife garden near Dorchester, designed and created by Peter and Pam Lewis; **66** Sarah Raven's Cutting Garden in Brightling, designed by Sarah Raven; **67** ph Caroline Hughes/Iden Croft Herbs; **68** Marc Schoellen's garden, 'La Bergerie', in Luxembourg; **69a** ph Caroline Hughes/Iden Croft Herbs; **69b** Fovant Hut Garden near Salisbury in Wiltshire was created by garden designer Christina Oates together with her husband Nigel and is open to the public; **70** Marc Schoellen's garden, 'La Bergerie', in Luxembourg; **72b** ph Francesca Yorke; **73** Fovant Hut Garden near Salisbury in Wiltshire was created by garden designer Christina Oates together with her husband Nigel and is open to the public; **74r** ph Pia Tryde; **75** ph Francesca Yorke; **76al** ph Caroline Hughes; **76bl & r** ph Andrea Jones; **77** ph Caroline Arber/Rosemary Titterington at Iden Croft Herbs; **78al** ph Chris Tubbs; **78bl, br & 79a** ph Pia Tryde; **79b** ph Andrea Jones; **80l** ph Pia Tryde; **80ar** ph Andrea Jones; **80–81b** Marc Schoellen's garden, 'La Bergerie', in Luxembourg; **81** ph Andrea Jones/Rowden Gardens; **82** a garden in south London designed by Roberto Silva; **83al** ph Andrew Wood; **83r both** Fiona Naylor and Peter Marlow's roof garden in London designed by Fiona Naylor and landscape architect Lindsey Whitelaw; **84–85** ph Catherine Gratwicke/Marja Walters—London, designed by Michael Reeves, Kauna mats from Ganesha, bamboo table from Emily Readett-Bayley, linen towels from Eastern Trading Allowance; **86** a garden in London designed by Jonathan Bell; **87** ph Andrew Wood/'Melwani House' designed by Bedmar & Shi designers in Singapore; **88l** garden of interior designer Suzanne Rheinstein, designed by Judy M. Horton; **88r** Laura Cooper and Nick Taggart's Los Angeles garden, designed by Cooper/Taggart Designs; **89l** Fiona Naylor and Peter Marlow's roof garden in London designed by Fiona Naylor and landscape architect Lindsey Whitelaw; **89r** ph Andrea Jones/Stoners; **90l** a garden in south London designed by Roberto Silva; **90–91 & 91c** ph Caroline Hughes/John and Joan Ward's garden in London; **91r** Mr. and Mrs. James Hepworth's garden in Herefordshire; **92–93** all ph Andrea Jones; **94** ph Chris Tubbs; **96r & 97**

© ph Steve Painter; **98** ph Christopher Drake/Mr. & Mme. Degrugillier, Le Mas de Flore, Antiquite et Creation, Lagnes, Isle sur Sorgue, Provence; garden table & chair, Le Mas de Flore; cushion, l'Utile e il Dilettevole; **99** ph Andrea Jones; **100** ph Christopher Drake/antique lanterns, l'Utile e il Dilettevole; **100–101** Elspeth Thompson's garden in south London; **101** ph Christopher Drake/Guido & Marilea Somarè's house in Milan; bamboo garden lamps, Habitat; **102** Fiona Naylor and Peter Marlow's roof garden in London designed by Fiona Naylor and landscape architect Lindsey Whitelaw; **103** ph Christopher Drake/Enrica Stabile's house in Provence; **104** ph Christopher Drake/Giorgio & Irene Silvagni's house in Provence; iron bed by Giorgio Silvagni at L'Utile e il Dilettevole; silk moiré cushion, L'Utile e il Dilettevole; **105l** ph Tom Leighton; **105r** the garden and nursery De Brinkhof of Riet Brinkhof & Joop Van Den Berk; **106l** Laura Cooper & Nick Taggart's Los Angeles garden designed by Cooper/Taggart Designs; **106r & 107l** Elspeth Thompson's garden in south London; **107r** ph Pia Tryde; **108** ph Andrea Jones/La Bambouserie de Prafrance; **110–111** ph Caroline Hughes/Iden Croft Herbs; **112–113** Sticky Wicket wildlife garden near Dorchester, designed and created by Peter and Pam Lewis; **114** ph Stephen Robson; **114–115** ph Caroline Hughes/Iden Croft Herbs; **115** ph Stephen Robson; **116** ph Caroline Hughes/Iden Croft Herbs; **117l** ph Caroline Hughes/HDRA's Yalding Organic Gardens, near Maidstone, Kent; **117r** ph Stephen Robson; **118** ph Anne Hyde; **119a** ph Francesca Yorke; **119b & 120l** ph Pia Tryde; **120c** ph Caroline Arber; **120–121** ph Caroline Hughes/Iden Croft Herbs; **122–127** ph Caroline Hughes; **128** Derry Watkins's garden in Wiltshire designed by Derry Watkins and her husband, the architect Peter Clegg; **129** ph Andrea Jones/Japanese Garden & Bonsai Nursery; **130l** Niall Manning & Alastair Morton's garden, Dunard, Fintry, Scotland G63 0EX; **130r** ph Jan Baldwin; **131** ph Andrew Wood/'Melwani House' designed by Bedmar & Shi designers in Singapore; **132–133** architect's house and garden in London designed by Dale Loth Architects; **134a** a house in Chelsea, lighting designed by Sally Storey; **134b** garden designed by Judy Kameon—Elysian Landscapes; **135** Sarah Harrison & Jamie Hodder-Williams's roof terrace in London designed by Stephen Woodhams; **136l** ph Andrea Jones; **136–137** Sticky Wicket wildlife garden near Dorchester, designed and created by Peter and Pam Lewis; **137** ph Andrea Jones/La Bambouserie de Prafrance.

Index

Page numbers in *italic* refer to the illustrations